Hans Gutbrod
Handbook for Professional Communication

AF206506

Handbook for Professional Communication

Third Edition

Hans Gutbrod

Bibliographic information published by the Deutsche Nationalbibliothek

The Deutsche Nationalbibliothek lists this publication in the Deutsche Nationalbibliografie; detailed bibliographic data are available on the Internet at http://dnb.dnb.de.

IMPRINT

Handbook for Professional Communication
by Hans Gutbrod

Author: Hans Gutbrod
Contact: hfgutbrod@gmail.com

Printed and Published by BoD - Books on Demand, Norderstedt, Germany

ISBN 978-3-7448-7078-8

A Shelf for Your Ideas – Preface to the Third Edition

In the 1930s, a young mother in Tbilisi was in a desperate situation. Her husband had been deported in one of Stalin's purges. She had a young child and with her husband being an enemy of the people, she had no source of income. She went to relatives and neighbors, asking for work. One of the neighbors eventually offered her to work as the math tutor for their son, who was coming into sixth grade. The young mother was petrified. She had only been in school for four years, yet needed the income to survive and feed her child. In her desperation, she accepted the job.

Once she began tutoring, she sat with the little boy, trying to work through the math problems in his book, and trying to hide that she was uncertain about the right solution. She thus encouraged the boy to figure it out: "dumai, dityë, dumai" – think, kid, think! Perpetually worried that she would be found out, she was told by the boy's parents, a few months later, that she was the best tutor that the child had ever had. Through her encouragement, he had figured it out, by himself.

This story, told by Natalia Antelava, a journalist and friend, about how her grandmother survived, in many ways is relevant to professional communication. Since writing the first edition of this book, in May 2001, I have taught the skill on how to structure information to more than 1500 people, in various settings, from four-day workshops to 90-minute summaries.

Practically all of the people in the trainings already have many good ideas on how to communicate. Many of the people are very good at figuring out how to structure information, when we go through practical examples.

Yet few of them have a worked-out approach on how to get their ideas across. Their understanding of the challenge often is

5

fragmentary. When we discuss, for example, how to structure introductions, most will have good ideas but not a developed framework. In some ways, it is like they have most of the right books yet no bookshelf to put them on. Their ideas, like such books, are in unordered piles. This makes them far less usable than they should be.

This handbook, then, tries to offer shelves: a framework for ideas on communication that give you a clear structure to work with. Ideas, like books, are much more useful if they are in good order.

I think it is fair to say that the framework presented here is one that has worked. At least it worked for me, in various settings, for example when we convinced dozens of think tanks around the world to become more transparent about who funds them. Others have also found the framework useful, which is why we are going into this third edition. Previous versions were published in Armenia, Bulgaria, Central America, Georgia, Mongolia, Ukraine and Russia, and versions of this handbook have been used for teaching students in Bamberg and Berlin.

Having a framework makes communication much easier. At the same time, what I present here is just one framework. I do think you will find useful to fully understand it, working through the tough parts, and to apply it. If afterwards you transcend it, developing additional ideas and approaches, that is even better. The handbook tries to give you a structure to figure it all out. In this, dumai, dityë, dumai has been a good motto for me. I hope it works for you as well.

This handbook extensively refers to Georgian examples, as Georgians are the primary audience of this version. Non-Georgian readers may enjoy the reference to a different context.

Contents

4321 – What you need to know before you start

What this book is for; how it can help you; how you should use it.

To live and actively participate in a society requires you to communicate all the time. This is why most people want to be better at communicating. Being better at communicating allows you to succeed and to help others succeed. You have a better chance of transmitting your ideas.

But it is difficult to learn professional communication. Universities rarely teach it in good courses. Without systematic teaching, there isn't an established framework for professional communication, or an ongoing discussion on how such a framework could look. And professional communication is not a skill that can easily be learned from a book.

So how can this book make a difference? I believe that this book can give you the tools to succeed: four principles, three structures, two formulas and one procedure. If you master them, you will do very well. You will first learn the four principles that always apply and then see how to put them into practice. Three structures help you make your ideas accessible. Two simple formulas will support you, and you can adapt them to your requirements. The book will also show you a procedure that you can always use to draft documents.

To make the most of this book I suggest that you thoroughly engage with its first part. It is short, for your benefit. You should fully understand the four principles, three structures, two formulas and one procedure. Once you have the 4321 framework internalized, you have the basics for practically all professional documents. We will discuss specific formats in the second part of the book.

The primary purpose is to get you to think in the right direction. You will need to think because you will need to make choices.

For that reason, the book is designed around transferable advice that you can adapt. Use this book as a tool that opens possibilities, not as a text that imposes constraints.

The handbook draws on the experience of running organizations, of working with think tanks across multiple countries, of campaigning with international impact, and of teaching and coaching. Moreover, it draws on the experience of making mistakes that I can help you avoid. I have used techniques that have been successful across many countries and various organizations, including the private and public sector and the military. The biggest inspiration has been Barbara Minto, who has put together some of the best ideas on how to write clearly. Throughout, however, I have tried to keep in mind what you, an interested reader, will find useful.

The 4321 Essentials

How to get started.

To communicate well, you need to follow four principles. These principles apply to all professional communication, and they also underlie the structure which we use to organize ideas. Your success will depend on your understanding of these essentials, and on your ability to apply them in various contexts. The following pages explain the four principles, three visualization techniques that help you build a structure, two formulas and a procedure which you will find useful whenever you write.

Four Principles

The principles that always apply whatever text you are writing.

- ***Define your purpose in writing***

Professional communication is about achieving results. You write so that something will or can happen. Whenever you write, clarify what result you are trying to bring about. Even if you just want to inform someone, you give them this information so that they can ask themselves whether they need to change or adapt their own plans in response to what you tell them. If you are sure that they do not need to act, most likely they do not need to know.

Hence define the purpose before you do anything else. One good way of defining the purpose is to create a visual image of the specific action you want your reader to take. When writing a memo, you want people at least to take note – which means that they should ask themselves and their subordinates the question "Do we agree with the proposed action? If we don't, what is our better suggestion on what to do?" When writing a CV, you usually want to obtain an invitation to the interview.

Consequently, you should picture the situation where the person looking at your CV compares it with the criteria for the position, decides that you are suitable, sets it aside and tells her assistant to invite you for an interview.

Who does what how when where why?

Having defined your image, write down the specific actions you want to happen as a result of your document. Be specific. The action formula for writing down the objective is: "Who does what how when where why?" This formula is used wherever people need to take decisions and implement them. As all action goals can be formulated in this way, you benefit from always using it.

Having the image and the written formula alone does not ensure that you will succeed. But if you do not create the image, you may fail to define your purpose and you will be even less likely to succeed. At the same time, the image helps you to check whether your aspiration is realistic. Can you visualize it happening? Have you seen something similar happen recently? If so, your goal probably is realistic. You will, of course, occasionally try something new that previously never happened – but these are exceptions. Usually you will want to pursue less ambitious goals, as doing so allows you to succeed more often.

- *Write for the reader*

Having established your visualized aim, pursue it by writing specifically for the reader. Who is the reader? Why is the reader reading your document? What are the reader's interests, expectations, beliefs and possibilities? I suggest characterizing the reader with three to five adjectives. Characterize before you begin to plan your document. Decide whether you need to do some research about your reader (or groups of readers).

The principle that you write for the reader guides you whenever you have to make a difficult decision about how your document should look. By asking yourself what would be best for the reader you focus your thoughts on the one criterion that counts. To make your document attractive, ask yourself just how much your reader needs to know. It is unprofessional to be longer than you need to be, as your typical reader faces many competing concerns. Too little detail, on the other hand, may leave the reader unable to decide, and may lead to further back-and-forth.

Remember that you yourself want documents (including this book) to be written so that they meet your needs. Do others the same favour. If you keep setting a good example in your organization, others will soon follow.

To understand the right approach, it helps to reflect on the difference between professional and other types of writing. Writing e-mails or messages to friends mostly is about expressing yourself. You do that in whichever way you want. You expect your friends to understand your style, as it reflects your feelings. Friendship at least in part is about understanding each other.

Professional communication is different. It has the purpose of achieving tangible results in an effective way. Unlike the communication between friends, its prime purpose is not that people should enjoy each other's company.

Note, too, the difference to literature. Literature entertains and at its best inspires us. If it is good it encourages various interpretations of its meaning. Its language often is complex, because decoding texts can be a thrill.

Professional communication is more narrowly strategic. You do not want multiple interpretations. Instead, readers should act. They must know precisely what you want to say. Your priority in the use of language should be clarity.

- *Present your conclusion first*

Present your main idea first. Only then introduce the ideas that support this main idea. In other words: state your conclusion first and then say why this is the right conclusion. Readers find it easier to understand your text if you follow that sequence.

Do not take the reader through your thought process. Taking the reader through your thinking takes more time and you may lose the attention of the person you are addressing. Consider the example:

> In the river Mtkvari: what would you use?
>
> Version 1 --- "You, listen to me and look over here, I'm not in a good situation and I cannot get out by myself so I think that you could be pretty important to me. I need you to take off your clothes, and your shoes too, now jump into the river and quickly swim in my direction. Then grab me and pull me out."
>
> Version 2 --- "Help!"

In the second version, having stated the main idea first, the listener knows what to do. You do not have to take him through every single point. The same is true for professional communication. If you communicate the main idea first, many of the details become obvious.

The extreme example illustrates a reality we often encounter in writing. While struggling in the river practically everyone will use a simple call for help. Yet often, when it comes to writing, people resort to the kind of convoluted message of the first version. Too much detail drowns out the core idea. Putting the main first helps to make sure this does not happen.

The principle of "main idea first" applies to all communication, unless there is a specific exception. You should use this principle in essays, in memos, in professional letters, when answering questions. You even use the principle when presenting options: you present the idea that there is a good choice between these specific alternatives and you make the case that there are no other viable courses of action. How it works in detail will be explained in the next section on structures.

There are some exceptions to this conclusion-first format. An obvious exception is most literature. Because she wants you to remain curious, Agatha Christie does not tell you right away who the murderer is. Moreover, for some professional documents you must pass on "neutral" information for other people to make their own choices. Here you must keep out your own ideas. We will discuss the exceptions in the section on formats. In the meantime, use every opportunity to apply the principle of main idea first to your writing.

- *Always think before you type & be precise*

Much of what has been said above can be summarised as "think before you type". Use paper and pencil to plan your documents. Your documents will be more compelling, clearer, and mostly shorter. You will increase your chances of success and save yourself frustration.

Thinking thoroughly before you type goes along with another principle: be precise. I could repeat this principle throughout this book but I hope that saying it once with emphasis is enough. Without precision, you cannot think well because your thoughts will remain vague: they cannot work together to generate substantial and authoritative results.

For example, when we want to get together we would never agree to "meet somewhere on David Agmaneshebeli some time Thursday afternoon". Yet, in professional contexts we often see documents that are vague on how institutions will work together and achieve results, only stating a broad intention to collaborate. Precision here can save much effort, in the same way that precise arrangements on where to meet will save us the effort of looking for each other.

To be effective, we can go back to the action formula, and specify who does what how when where why. Specifying these aspects early greatly assists your planning, and your writing. Note that precision is a great tool to get ahead, within and between organizations. You have a good chance of prevailing if you continue being more precise, even against the odds. Precision, as the story of David's victory over Goliath illustrates, is a powerful weapon for the underdog.

- ***The hierarchy of the four principles***

Keep the four principles above in mind. They follow from each other. If you have a purpose and a clear image of what you want the reader to do, you automatically want to write for the reader. If you write for the reader, you will structure the text so that it is easy to understand. You will put the main idea in the beginning. And you will spend more time planning your documents in the future, thinking first so that you can save yourself work later.

The relationship of the principles is hierarchical, with the higher principles dominating over the lower ones: if you have diverse readers (Second Principle) with potentially contradicting views, you may sacrifice precision (Fourth Principle). This is what advertisements or political slogans do, deliberately targeting their messages to a diverse audience. The term "compassionate conservatism" used in the US presidential election in 2000 is perhaps one of the most powerful examples. The term was finely crafted to send two different messages: to mostly secular voters in the middle of the political spectrum it can sound like conservatism distinguished by moderation (it appears compassionate, not tough); to committed Christians it sounds like an emphasis on Christian doctrine (with policies against what they see as liberal excess).

Similarly, if your reader (Second Principle) is negatively disposed to your conclusions, you may decide not to begin by putting your main idea first (Third Principle), but instead show that all other options have been exhausted. Moreover, if your purpose is to convince (First Principle) readers who may feel threatened (Second Principle) by your main message, you will demonstrate and establish your empathy first, removing or at least reducing their anxiety before delivering your main message. As these examples illustrate, the principles give you a robust structure for thinking about communication.

Writing is like building a house. Texts structure meaning in the way that buildings structure space. Both ventures tend to succeed if they are accessible, rather than labyrinthine. For both, if they are more than emergency cover, you need to plan sensibly, putting different materials together in a single unit. Good writing like good building is primarily about planning. Typing is like laying bricks: necessary for completion, but unlikely to deliver desirable results without a solid plan. The next sections will give you some more advice on how to assemble the plan for successful communication.

Three Structures

How to organize your ideas.

To write professional documents you need to know how to organize them. The entire structure flows from the third principle: present your conclusion first. This presentation principle helps you to structure your thoughts. In this section, you will learn an approach that allow you to present any material to your reader. Once you master this technique, you can apply it consistently to develop any type of document.

Throughout this section, we will be referring to the example presented below.

- **State the main idea first**

We have already determined that you should present your conclusion in the beginning, as it helps the reader understand what you are saying. To illustrate this principle, let us examine the example below. Read it and try to identify the differences for yourself before you read on.

Memo to Nino, the director of a marketing consultancy, written by Paata, after several clients turned down proposed projects. Two versions:

> Version 1 --- Giorgi was unhappy with the way our project pipeline is going. He says he has too much work on existing projects, he cannot concentrate on personnel, legal aspects and completing the pitches to clients at the same time, especially as he also has to take Keti's position whenever she is away. He is already late with the yearly review because it is too much.
>
> I discussed it with Keti. She says she can't help Giorgi, because she needs all the time to focus on maintaining

17

the contacts with clients. As no one else is available, Giorgi and Keti think that we should consider employing an assistant to concentrate on completing our pitches. Giorgi would be responsible for the assistant. The assistant would probably cover her cost, as we would have better chances of getting more income if someone had more time to spend on it. Could we meet this Thursday 15:00 to discuss this with you and Irakli? Thanks, Paata

Version 2 --- Giorgi and Keti suggest hiring a junior assistant to increase our sales. We would like to meet you and Irakli this Thursday 15:00-16:00 in your office to discuss this proposal.

A dedicated assistant will be able to help complete pitches that clients are interested in, and potentially additional clients. This move seems necessary after we missed out on several pitches recently. If we succeed in winning more projects, we could expect the assistant to cover the costs of employing her and to earn additional income for the company.

Moreover, having this assistant would allow Giorgi – who would supervise her – to fully concentrate on existing projects, personnel and legal issues, allowing him to respond to more requests. This increased efficiency would enable us to take on further contracts, earning us some more money. With sufficient training the assistant would also be able to stand in for Keti, giving Keti more time to work on implementation with our clients. In terms of cost [add detail…].

Please let me know if the above is a convenient time for you to discuss this proposal.

Which version do you find more convincing?

Version 2 is better because it immediately tells the reader the main idea. The boss knows that Giorgi and Keti want to meet with her to discuss the hiring of an assistant on Thursday at 15:00. Writing for the reader, the author dropped several items that Version 1 – which takes the reader through the thought process – kept. Even if Version 1 were streamlined, the reader still would have difficulties understanding the text because she does not know to what conclusion it leads.

Note how the action formula ("who does what how when where why?") has been adapted to highlight the main point. The action formula would have been:

- Giorgi and Keti [who] want to discuss the hiring of a sales assistant with you and Irakli [what how] Thursday 15:00-16:00 [when] in your office [where] because creating this position should increase our revenue [why].

In Version 2 the formula was split into two sentences and the main idea was stated first. We instinctively understand things best if the main idea is presented first. The other supporting ideas fall into place.

This top-down principle is universally true because we process information from an organising principle. Having understood the central idea, we find it easy to remember the subordinate ideas. Think of a car and you can immediately visualise a lot of different components that fit together to make the vehicle. Conversely, if I tell you: door, window, roof, mirrors, seats, lights – you may think of a car, but you cannot be sure. Is it a house? Nor are you thinking of the many other parts of the car.

Always find the main idea – which should relate to the purpose of writing the document – and mention it in the beginning.

- *Structure the levels of your argument*

A complex argument may include several different ideas on different levels. You should put these ideas into an order that reveals their connections, thereby making them intelligible and compelling to the reader. The arrangement of these ideas is comparable to the order that you would develop in any collection of objects or ideas. For example, when arranging books on a shelf, you sort them by criteria and by sub-criteria (alphabetical order, subject area, size, or even colour). These criteria need to be used consistently, otherwise your order will be confusing to others.

The same is true for ideas. Take time to identify what your main idea is. From now on, we will call this main idea your thesis. Your thesis should be supported by further ideas, which we will call arguments. These arguments in turn will be supported by subarguments.

To work with such a structure, you should visualize what it looks like. There are three approaches to visualizing your structure that I have found useful: the argumentative circle, the pyramid, and the mind map. You can choose whichever you feel most comfortable with. Each has advantages and disadvantages.

The argumentative circle looks like a spider's web. In the center is your thesis. On the next level are your arguments. Beyond that come the subarguments and if what you are saying is very detailed, there will be supports. The argumentative circle looks awkward when printed, but is effective in dividing a page that is sideways in landscape format, with a pencil.

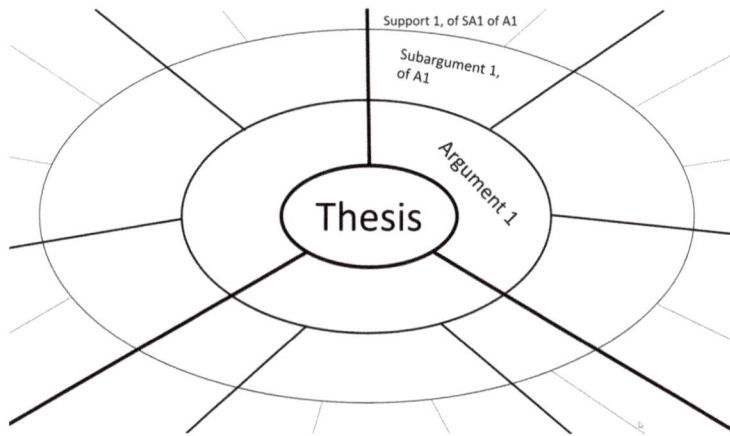

Support 1, of SA1 of A1

Subargument 1, of A1

Argument 1

Thesis

The pyramid is another visualization you can use. This top-down approach has been put forward by Barbara Minto. At the top, there is the thesis, on the next level you have the arguments, below the subarguments, and then the supports. The pyramid is a great way of envisaging information, and works particularly well if you use Post-it notes for planning on a big wall. The pyramid is less suitable for planning complex documents on a single piece of paper, because you run out of space on the lowest level, where you have all the detail. (Even on this page we struggle to include the subargument level.) To fit everything onto a page, the argumentative circle is more useful, as you branch out the detail to the edges of the paper. A single sheet with an argumentative circle holds information for planning a paper of 8 to 10 pages, or for a talk that lasts for an hour.

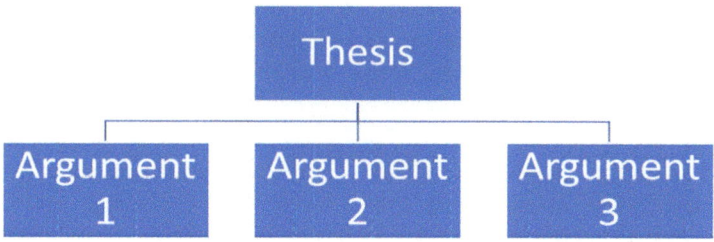

Thesis

| Argument 1 | Argument 2 | Argument 3 |

The mind map is the third useful visualization tool. The mind map has more of a flowing structure, in which the thesis sits in the central circle, and branches out to other items around it. The mind map, developed by Tony Buzan, is intuitive and engaging to draw and develop. Self-drawn mind maps are nicer to work with than the ones we get from computer programs, such as the one below. The one disadvantage of the mind map is that it has less of a rigorous emphasis on the hierarchical nature of your structure. Robust relationships often are represented more rigorously by the pyramid or the argumentative circle.

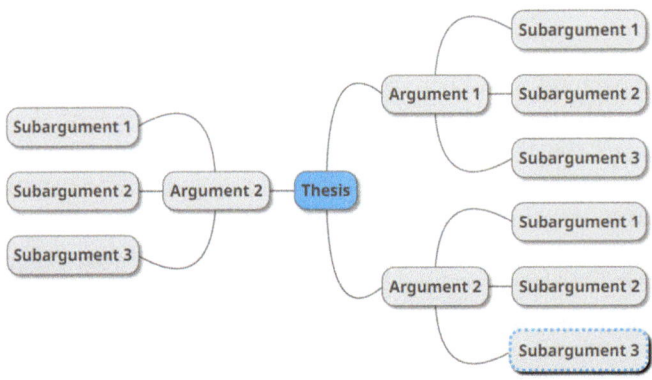

With these three visualizations tools, you can order complex information to make it accessible to others and to yourself. Make sure that the levels cohere in all directions. The thesis must be a summary of all the main arguments. And this structure then works all the way down (or out): the arguments must directly be supported by the subarguments. And the subarguments should be summaries of your supports.

The summaries must be "clean". Clean means that only ideas (i.e. arguments, subarguments, etc.) that directly contribute to this summary should be included. You can, for example, have reasons for greatly decreasing income tax and abolishing value-

22

added-tax as part of your case. (Your thesis could be: Ukraine needs to introduce two changes in its tax regime immediately in order to stimulate its economy, increase tax income, and decrease the shadow economy.) But in this context, you cannot make a point about altering the exchange rate (unless it directly relates). It simply does not add to your summary as expressed in the thesis.

The circle must cohere "sideways". If you have mentioned income tax and value-added-tax on the argument level, a decrease of tax on medicines against asthma does not fit on this level, as this topic is less significant to the overall thesis (and offers a greater level of detail than needed). You should, in other words, have roughly similar importance on each respective level. Our memo on the sales assistant can illustrate the requirement of coherence.

> Thesis:
> We should discuss the hiring of an assistant for project-pitches to increase our income.[1]
>
> Arguments
> 1.) She should be able to increase our revenue because she can concentrate on developing pitches.
> 2.) She will allow Giorgi to obtain more contracts because he can concentrate on his job.
> 3.) She can help to improve our service by freeing Keti to spend time with her clients.

Here all three arguments highlight the possibility of generating more income: by improving efficiency and quality, you are likely to stimulate demand, as your products or services become more attractive relative to other offers. The proposed change should

---

[1] This thesis still is an abbreviated action formula. It is implicit that "us" refers to specific people and that the meeting should take place at a certain time and place.

generate more income, of course, because otherwise the organization cannot afford to pay for the new assistant. The three arguments are roughly on the same level of importance. It is right that they are mentioned together, and at the argument level.

Now, try to imagine an argument that does <u>not</u> belong here. One clear example of such a misfit is:

- She can remind Giorgi to return his coffee cups to the kitchen, because Giorgi always forgets to do it, makes a mess, and no one else has cups left.

While this may be true, the argument would not be on the same level as the other three arguments. Coffee cups are not important enough and their return does not contribute to the revenue collection of the consultancy. Hence they should not be included. It would, however, be permissible to say:

- She can increase efficiency by taking charge of Giorgi's office management.

This statement coheres with the other three arguments. The other three arguments were about a possible increase in income due to employing an assistant. Improving office management is about decreasing cost, as internal processes will go more quickly and hence cost less. So all four arguments are about the same activity: increasing revenue.

The argument about increased efficiency may include the *subargument* that the assistant will ensure that the office remains tidy, but it will also entail a range of other tasks, for example, managing the filing system. If the subargument is just about the office running out of coffee cups, you better drop it altogether.

All this means that a proper structure can be presented like a mathematical equation, with A standing for "argument":

Thesis $= A_1 + A_2 + A_3$
$A_1 =$ Subargument$_1$ of A_1 + Subargument$_2$ of A_1 + Subargument$_3$ of A_1

and so on.

The mathematical representation emphasizes that there should not be anything on the subargument level that is not reflected in the thesis, since the thesis is the sum of all the subarguments. Conversely, the arguments need to literally "add up" to present the content of the thesis. It is a rigorous, robust and fully rational structure.

Yet to fully grasp that structure, especially if you have more than four or five ideas that need to be integrated simultaneously, you will need to visualize it in one way or another, at the very least in a detailed outline form. Even better, use the argumentative circle, or the pyramid, or the mind map, to visualize your eventual structure.

- ***Pick 3-5 main points***

When organising items or arguments into a structure, you should ideally pick three to five main arguments. All other ideas should be subordinate on a level below as subarguments. Remember that you are writing for your readers. Their time is limited. If you identify three to five main arguments that are powerful, you should be able to convince them. If they are not convinced by these arguments, further arguments are unlikely to succeed.

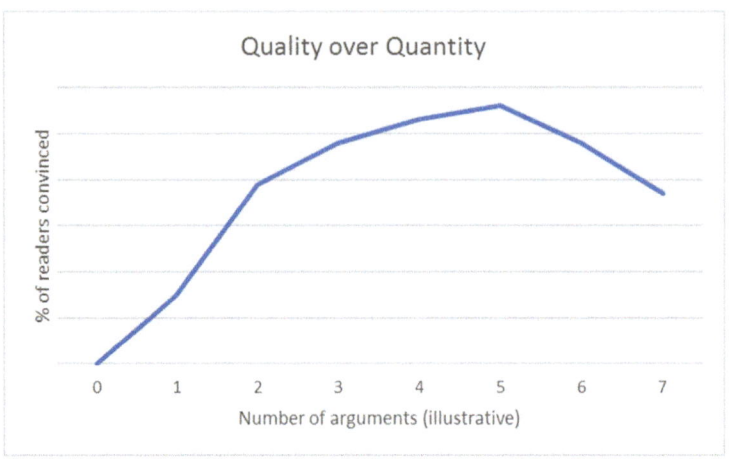

Quality over Quantity

% of readers convinced (y-axis)

Number of arguments (illustrative) (x-axis: 0 1 2 3 4 5 6 7)

One poor argument gives people who are sceptical a pretext for not listening to the other good arguments. They focus their objections on the one poor argument, disregarding the others. A poor argument increases the vulnerability of your document. Moreover, if your document lists all the arguments you can think of, it will be so long that nobody will want to read it.

Figure 2 shows how many readers are convinced relative to the number of arguments. The curve is illustrative and its actual shape will depend on the readers and the text. The point to remember is that quantity cannot substitute for the quality of a few well-chosen arguments.

You need to choose. Which arguments will you pick? The answer is to be found in the principles discussed above. Write for your reader: pick the arguments, then, that are most likely to make your reader act the way you want her to. As Nino needs to generate income to keep her company going, the main arguments in the short memo were well chosen.

- *Visualize processes, too*

Obviously, you can use any of these visualizations to describe a process, too. As "arguments" you have the main steps that need to be taken. Try to keep to the maximum of five steps. Five steps are easy to remember. Include further items as subarguments. Again, your levels should cohere. To use a straightforward example:

> Thesis:
> Keti, Paata and Giorgi will re-organize the office under Keti's leadership on Saturday at 09:00, because we need to create space for a new sales assistant
>
> Arguments:
> 1.) Discard all unneeded papers
> 2.) Re-arrange bookshelves
> 3.) Remove old sofa
> 4.) Set up new workspace.

Note that for each of those arguments there are subarguments, so that again you could fill the argumentative circle:

> 1.) Discard all unneeded papers:
>   a.)   Collect all loose paper
>   b.)   Identify what is needed and file accordingly
>   c.)   Identify confidential/private material to be discarded and shred it
>   d.)   Discard the rest
> etc.

Basically, you can put any activity that has a specific purpose into this format. It will help you plan and coordinate complex activities. Remember to visualise the purpose and to put it down as an action formula.

- *Put arguments into an appropriate sequence*

Put the arguments into the sequence that is most likely to appeal to the reader. Once you have a sequence, stay consistent. In other words: within a document you cannot vary the principle that determines the sequence of your arguments. Within the same document, however, you can vary the sequence in which you arrange different sets of subarguments.

In practice this could mean that if you write a book about what is distinctively Georgian about certain authors, you may want to dedicate one chapter to each author. Within each chapter, you will have a logical structure that will not vary *within* the chapter, although you may choose a different sequence for different chapters (i.e., the chapter on Galaktion Tabidze may be chronological, charting his development, while the chapter on Ilia Chavchavadze may discuss the significance of his work to five other Georgian authors).

This point will become even clearer when we look at different types of organizing ideas. In her book, Minto identifies four possible types of ordering (ordering as in DAGOR, a step-by-step planning process which I will explain later):

1.) Chronological: suitable for a process in which you describe a sequence of steps. A simple example are the office re-organization steps mentioned above.

2.) Structural: relates to separate parts of the organization, persons or locations – e.g., Legal, Accounting, Marketing; Giorgi, Keti, Paata; Batumi, Kutaisi, Tbilisi.

3.) Comparative: order the arguments according to how they measure up to a criterion. Usually you sort them by importance/relevance. Normally, you want to put the more important reasons in the beginning, otherwise the reader gets into the habit of rejecting your ideas and will not take your last arguments seriously. Look at the sample memo: it emphasizes generating income as the main function of the assistant they consider hiring. The additional administrative functions are secondary and are mentioned later.

4.) Deductive: basically, this is a syllogism. First make a major, true statement, followed by a minor statement that refers to the same issue or activity, and then combine the two. For example: (1) This book teaches you to communicate professionally. (2) You want to communicate professionally. (3) Hence you should read this book.

You should avoid using this deductive type of structure for longer expositions, as it violates the principle that you should state your conclusion first. The syllogism or deduction takes the reader through your thought process. Use instead: Read this book if you want to learn how to communicate professionally.

Decide what order is appropriate. For theses that argue why something is the case, the order should be Comparative or Structural – you do not tell a story or describe a process. For a process – describing "how" something is done, you should use Chronological or Structural. You can also use Comparative ("this is the most profitable activity"), but the comparison risks muddling the discussion of who should act, and at what point in the process. You can use the Deductive structure on the lowest level within a document, for example at the subargument level: to argue that the argument on lower cost will come about as a consequence of (1) and (2).

Almost everyone feels the temptation to go for the deductive organization at some point. Its attraction is that it allows you to give the larger setting first, then to describe the situation before you come to a conclusion. The informed reader can make her own judgments. Such a sequence would seem particularly logical when you comment on someone else's work.

As mentioned above, this overall deductive structure only works in short documents which remain on the argument level without getting into any substantial subarguments. If the discussion goes deeper, the deductive structure becomes too complex. Setting out the basic context may take several pages. Elaborating such basics is boring because the reader does not know what exactly he eventually will need the knowledge for. What is even more problematic is that the reader is likely to forget the relevant information before it becomes relevant again.

Let us imagine that you are trying to correct what you consider to be some misinterpretations in Irakli's report about the situation in Svaneti, Megrelia and Guria. If you use the deductive method on the argument level, you will first present a summary of what Irakli has reported (major premise). You will then describe the actual situation (minor premise) as you see it. You then conclude that some interpretations in Irakli's report need to be corrected.

Now imagine that Irakli has included a survey of the current situation in the society, administration, and economy. Can you see the problem? To summarize his report, you will have nine distinct items of information (society, administration and economy each in the three regions). By the time you get to give your own comments, the reader will have forgotten what exactly it was that Irakli was saying about administration in Guria.

Therefore you must push the deductive order down to the lowest possible level. Conversely, you bring the actual issues up to the argument level. It is a quick and easy switch, which may sound more complicated than it is. Let us quickly walk through this process. Previously you had roughly the following sequence:

> Thesis (abbreviated): Although a comprehensive foundation for our policy proposal, three aspects of Irakli's survey need to be amended.

30

Irakli's interpretation
(subargument: Svaneti, Megrelia, Guria)

Actual situation
(subargument: Svaneti, Megrelia, Guria)

Conclusion about Irakli's misinterpretation
(subargument: Svaneti, Megrelia, Guria).

This structure, as mentioned, has the disadvantage that specific information about the regions becomes relevant at three different points in the paper, without any strong connection.

Now, having pushed the deductive order down to the subargument, you have the following structural order, according to regions (thesis omitted):

Irakli's optimistic misinterpretation of Svaneti
(subargument: Irakli, the actual situation, conclusion)

Irakli's overly pessimistic misinterpretation of Megrelia
(subargument: Irakli, the actual situation, conclusion)

Irakli's partial misinterpretation of the economic potential in Guria
(subargument: Irakli, the actual situation, conclusion).

You still give the reader the context, but you do so where it becomes most relevant. If necessary, you push the deductive sequence even further down to the support level. If, for example, Irakli had indeed written about the economy, the administration and society in each region, you could use each of them as your subarguments, putting the detailed discussion of Irakli's misinterpretation onto the support level.

This is how it could look:

> Argument$_1$: Irakli's optimistic misinterpretation of Svaneti
>> Subargument$_1$: the optimistic view of the Svan economy
>>> Support level: Irakli, the actual situation, conclusion
>>
>> Subargument$_2$: the optimistic view of administrative reform in Svaneti
>>> Support level: Irakli, the actual situation, conclusion
>
> Argument$_2$: [...]
>
>> and so on for the remaining arguments and subarguments and supports.

You could also use another order, according to topics (economy, society, administration), rather than regions. Your decision will primarily depend on whether you can identify shared characteristics that can be summarized on the argument level. In other words, if Irakli is entirely right in what he says about the economy, completely wrong in his statements about the administration, and not relevant in what he says about society, you can use this pattern to structure your criticisms.

Note that this wonderful trick – again one that I learnt from Minto – always works and will make papers much more readable, as well as easier to write.

- *It's all about structure*

I cannot emphasize enough how important a clean structural setup is. Sometimes when I talk about structure in trainings, I see people's eyes glaze over, as if this concern is not relevant to them. Of course, the challenge is on me to make it exciting. At the same time, I am often asked to come in and repair reports that made these basic structural mistakes. Let me mention two of those as warning examples. In one case, a colleague proposed the following structure for a report on increasing employment opportunities for Internally Displaced Persons (IDPs):

Structure of the Report on IDP Employment

I. Background, methodology and literature review
  1. Past studies on Georgia's workforce
  2. Relevant literature and lessons from other NIS countries
  3. Summary of literature on IDP livelihoods in Georgia
II. Demographic and geographic characterization of IDPs, and employment characteristics
III. Labour supply: Participation in the labour force
  1. Urban (self-employed, informal wage employed, formal wage employed, unemployed, inactive)
  2. Rural – same categories as above, including agriculture/farming
IV. Labour demand: Overview and characteristics of employment opportunities
  1. Urban (formal and informal sectors)
  2. Rural (focusing mostly on informal sectors)
V. Best practices and lessons learned from Georgia and the NIS
VI. Recommendations to the State Civic Unit and suggestions for further research

If you have read the previous section, you will immediately identify what the problem is. As a test, see whether you can spot it.

The structural problem is with Section III and Section IV, respectively. The topics should be switched to subargument level, with urban and rural becoming the organizing units, instead of supply and demand. We then have urban labour supply and demand, and rural labour supply and demand, as the connection between those is what is relevant when we look at employment. Other changes should be made, too: the demographics could be included in a characterization of labor supply and demand, since this is where the information is most relevant. Arguably, even parts of Section I could be folded in, and the methodology could be at the end.

In another example, an organization looked at attitudes towards ongoing reform. For sake of simplicity, let us say they were looking at educational reform, using a survey of teachers, focus groups with teachers, and a survey of parents. They then presented the results by research instrument.

Choosing this structure, with three different research instruments on the argument level, meant that they covered the same issue (say: hiring) three times, in various parts of the report. Thus, to understand the findings, per issue, you had to go back and forth. The report was not publishable, and needed to be fixed. Weeks passed while the report needed to be restructured, even though the report was of intense interest to the institutions that were involved.

Incidentally, often a giveaway for such structural challenges is the word "above-mentioned". If this word is used several times, it likely is an indication of a structural flaw in the document, as text should flow naturally, without needing to refer back up.

If you can contribute to avoiding such mistakes, potentially using visualizations to help your colleagues understand how to make a text more accessible, you will do your institution a great service. Once you have mastered structure, you have what you need to write robust and compelling documents.

Introduction Formula

How to write any introduction.

It is generally recognized that good introductions help to make documents successful. Many people, however, find it difficult -- almost painful -- to write them. Fortunately, there is a formula for good introductions.[2] This formula can be applied to all introductions – in long reports, short letters, and you can even use it to begin a speech. Bear in mind that the writing of introductions has two purposes.

First, your introduction should engage your audience. You should draw in your readers and convince them to read on. You should tell the reader what question your document will answer. As such, your main idea or thesis should be included. An introduction is similar to an overture to an opera – it establishes a setting, provides context, motives and themes/melodies that will follow.

Second, working on your introduction is an occasion for checking your plan for the entire document. Because you tell the reader what question you will answer, the planning of your introduction helps you to refine your purpose, to reflect on your structure and content, and to add improvements.

- **Standard SCQR-formula**

Here is the formula, abbreviated with SCQR: Situation, Complication, Question, Resolution.

Start by describing a standard situation that the reader is familiar with. Write inclusively, in describing an issue in terms that all (or

---

[2] This formula has been put forward by Barbara Minto, who developed it from Cleanth Brooks and Robert Penn Warren, *Fundamentals of Good Writing*, New York: Harcourt, 1950.

almost all) readers can agree with. Then show that a complication arises. The complication raises a question and your document offers the resolution.[3]

If Paata were to write a formal proposal, its introduction could look like this:

> Sixty percent of our consultancy's income relies on funding which we obtain for specific projects. In the last six months, however, we have lost five competitions for well-funded projects, at least three of which we should have won. How can we improve our project pitches? This proposal suggests that we should hire an assistant, to increase our sales.

Remember from the above memo, that Nino, Paata's main reader, is familiar with the situation. The introduction sets out that Paata and Nino agree on what the problem is, before moving to a proposed solution.

Look at how we started this book.

> To live and actively participate in a society requires you to communicate all the time. This is why most people want to be better at communicating. Being better at communicating allows you to succeed and to help others succeed. You have a better chance of transmitting your ideas. But it is difficult to learn professional communication. Universities rarely teach it in good courses. Without systematic teaching, there isn't an established framework for professional communication, or an ongoing discussion on how such a framework could look. And it is not a skill that can easily be learned

---

[3] In essence it applies ancient dialectical rhetoric: thesis (what is), antithesis (what challenges the thesis and the situation) joining to form the synthesis (what resolves the problem and reconciles thesis and antithesis).

from a book. So how can this book make a difference? I believe this book can give you the tools to succeed: four principles, three structures, two formulas and one procedure. If you master them, you will do very well...

You will recognize that the introduction of the book followed the SCQR- formula:

S – It is a fact that participation in a society requires you to communicate all the time. Similarly, it is generally true that most people want to improve their communication skills, because they recognize it as the key to success. Perhaps even everybody wants to be better at communicating – but as some people might object ("well, for example, my grand-uncle in remote Svaneti...") we have put "most" – making it a statement that is difficult to object to.

C – But several complications arise – inadequate teaching at universities (which is a problem in many countries, as successful communicators rarely stay to teach at university), and thus no established framework people draw on, difficulty of learning something like this from a book.

Q – The complication raises the question that must be of prime concern to you, the reader: how can this book make a difference?

R – Our resolution presents the main ideas first: if you know the four principles, three structures, two formulas and one procedure, you have all you really need. You then merely need to apply this to the specific document templates.

As you can see, the formula provides a structure that guides the reader towards the point that you seek to convey.

- *Flexibility*

The great thing about the SCQR formula (Situation, Complication, Question, Resolution) is that it is flexible because you can adapt it to different purposes by changing its sequence:

Action oriented: RCS

> "We should retrain staff in project-management skills. Julie, who has run very successful project-management training events for us in the past, has offered to prepare and run three half-day workshops, with a special focus on project planning in mid-April. This seminar should help us to improve work after several projects ran into difficulties and delays, causing additional costs and friction with clients, mostly due to elementary planning mistakes. As our organization's margins depends on keeping our clients satisfied, we need to ensure that project planning runs as smoothly as possible."

Dramatic: CSR

> "Our company is in a perilous state. In the last two months, three of our five biggest clients have expressed dissatisfaction with how we have run projects, complaining about severe delays and overly optimistic planning. We had additional costs, as we hired additional consultants to address clients' concerns. The combination of dissatisfied clients and cost-overruns threatens our revenue, and the intended investments. We should therefore retrain staff in project management skills, and especially in project planning. Julie, who has run very successful training events for us in the past, has kindly offered to prepare and run a three half-day workshops in mid-April."

"How will we resolve the crisis in our company? Our organization depends on satisfied clients, since our top five clients account for 80% of our revenue. But three of the five top clients currently are unhappy, complaining about delays and "sloppy" planning by our teams. We should therefore retrain staff in project management, with an emphasis on accurate planning, to address this issue and ensure our clients receive a service that meets the highest standards. Julie, who has run successful project management trainings for us, has kindly offered to prepare and run three half-day workshops in mid-April."[4]

Choose the one that is suitable for your purpose and your specific readers. If you want to be direct, use RSC (or RCS). This resolution-first sequence follows the principle of stating the main idea first. Its disadvantage is that it may appear too bossy. Some readers prefer to understand the setting before they start getting into the problem or being told about the solution, making SCQR the default option. This sequence can come across as thoughtful and ordered.

You can test the validity of the formula by checking texts you like. You will encounter this structure in compelling writing, including magazine articles. The SCQR is more than just an instrument for introductions: it is the basic structure of a dramatic plot, which moves from a general situation to a crisis, and then is resolved. What unites both comedy and tragedy is that what initially appears as a resolution turns into the next complication. At its heart the formula expresses a basic dialectical structure, familiar to ancient Greeks: thesis, its anti-

---

[4] Missing from this example is more detail on the workshop, including what staff think of this idea, and what the cost of this workshop will be.

thesis, and a synthesis which unites, resolves and transcends the juxtaposition.

To illustrate its broad applicability, the table below shows how some well-known ways of beginning a speech are a part of the SCQR framework.

Various ways of beginning a speech

	S	C	Q	Comment & Risks
Anecdote "A few weeks ago I was visiting a hazelnut plantation in Samegrelo, when …"	XX	X		- May not relate - Can turn off, if not done well - Too long for use many written texts, except for articles
Shared Experience "Eight years ago many of us in this room were shocked / surprised / delighted …"	XX			- Can help connect speaker and audience - Can also relate to current event that is on people's mind - Needs tob e authentic to work
Listener Motivation "Most of you are here today to help identify practical mechanisms to increase the quality of internal communication in …"	XX	X		- Can establish a shared concern as the situation, and highlight that the speaker understands the needs oft he audience
Amazing Fact "More than 75 % of Georgian women actually think that …"	X	XX		- Small if you have done good research
Puzzle "Why is it that despite all the difficulties XYZ still functions?"		X	X	- Small if you pose a credible and intriguing question
Rhetorical question "What ist he most important feature for our online customers?"			XX	

Quotation "As Kvachi Kvachantiradze in Mikhail Javakhisvhili's novel says when …"	XX			- Likely to bore if the speaker neglects her own ideas
Joke "A minister, a policeman an a businesswoman are sitting in heaven …"	X			- Risky because the joke fails if you get off to a bad start - Unless it is particularly compelling and tested with audiences, better to avoid
Statistics "In the last five years the average age of XY has increased by YZ …"	X			- Ideally turned into memorable fact or puzzle

In writing and professional communication, I have found SCQR one of the single most useful instruments. The formula has helped me to achieve impact, with various documents. Since discovering it, more than 15 years ago, I probably use it 3-4 times a week. Taken together, I have probably used it more than 2.500 times, over the years, not counting teaching and training. I have also used it in emergency situations, for example when arriving at what I thought was a small event to find the room filled with media representatives, and having to make a cogent statement in front of several TV cameras. The formula may be similarly useful to you.

To use the introduction formula successfully requires practice, easily 40-50 instances or more before you become comfortable with it. Once you have a knack for the formula, it becomes easy to draft attractive openers or introductions for yourself or others. In your practice, watch out to make sure that your situation and complication are appropriately succinct. In many trainings, participants create situations that are too vague. The action formula can help to achieve precision, and wordings that put people front and centre. Similarly, make sure your wording of the situation is inclusive, so that opponents in a bitter struggle could still agree with the way you describe the situation.

One last test is to visualize your introduction. Can you draw the situation, complication and resolution up in a few images? The visualization can help you clarify what you are trying to convey. With a clear visualization, you make sure that you describe a real problem that is connected to the situation, with the same people acting, or the same actions having an impact. By tightening your introduction, you also further focus your document.

Next to the action formula (who does what how when where why?), the introduction formula (SCQR) is the second formula you can use in writing, over and over again.

The DAGOR Procedure

How to proceed with planning any document.

DAGOR is a formula that you may find valuable whenever you have to plan a complicated text. Complicated texts are those with more than three separate ideas. Most people can easily structure two or three distinct ideas at a time. Once there are more than three related-yet-separate ideas, you need to plan to make these ideas accessible. The more ideas need to be integrated, and the less pre-structured they are, the more important planning becomes. DAGOR helps you to develop that plan.

I always use DAGOR. I used it for writing this guide, for articles, for more than 200 professional reports and project proposals, as well as for writing a dissertation. Some of the things that I will say now repeat what you have heard before. Partially this repetition comes about because this section should also be accessible for people who may not have looked at the previous sections in detail. Yet, we should anyway go back to the basic ideas. For we are now at the stage where we put the principles into action, and see how they work.

- *Think before you type*

Whatever else you do, think before you start writing. You will need paper and pencil to plan and visualize your structure, and should only start typing once you have finished planning.[5] Working more slowly at first, by planning in detail, will save you much time later.

-----

[5] Some people find digital planning tools useful. Several are available. I have used Scrivener, but otherwise prefer the large size of tables or even walls to the constraints of the screen. Moreover, it's refreshing to use alternatives to the computer.

- *DAGOR:*
  Define // Assemble // Group // Organize // Review

DAGOR is a simple and useful procedure –

> Define the purpose
> Assemble the ideas and information
> Group the ideas
> Organize an ordering structure
> Review your results.

The purpose of this procedure is to offer you a tool with which you can develop sophisticated, meaningful, balanced and concise documents. DAGOR can also help you improve or fix documents that still fall short. Conversely, if you encounter a badly written document, you can typically assume that the author did not know this procedure, or did not follow it.

Defining is about identifying the purpose. As I described in the sections on principles, you should create a visual image and articulate it in your action formula. Emphasize specific results that you want to achieve. Narrowing down allows you to concentrate your energy on well-defined and limited goals. It is better to apply much energy to a small challenge than to set yourself a problem that is too big to be tackled. Do not aim to construct two palaces when you only have material, time and energy to construct one solid house (which in most cases is all you need). Part of being successful is to recognise limitations – and then to fully exploit up to this limit.[6]

---

[6] When I am asked for advice on Master's theses, in the overwhelming majority of cases I find that students are tackling a topic for a Ph.D. dissertation. People writing Ph.D.s mostly are writing 4-5 dissertations at a time. I made the same mistake. A tight focus makes life (and writing) easier.

You also want to adapt this goal specifically to your reader, characterized by 3-5 adjectives, and define what interests different readers may share. As you cannot cover all aspects, identify those that are most relevant to your most important readers and that are most representative of the whole problem.

What you do here, in other words, is to set yourself the questions that you are trying to answer by putting the document together.

Assemble the information. Find out what is available and try to *make* ideas available: try to think of all you can. If you work in a group, have everyone sit in silence and write down their ideas for five minutes, and subsequently discuss ideas and try to generate more ideas.[7] Snowballing ideas allows less obvious ideas to surface and quieter members of the group to contribute. The emphasis here is on quantity, rather than on quality. Even if you are by yourself, you must write down all your ideas, otherwise the next item of information that you gather will displace them.

Do not start to write once you have your first idea. Rushing into writing at this point is like starting to build because you have found a supply of bricks and some cement: heroic but pointless. Both the document and the building need systematic and sustained planning if they are to be more than piles of words or bricks.

Group your ideas sensibly. What belongs together? The groups should describe the same object or the same activity. "I learned basic Chinese, I studied financial journalism, and I also learned how to write essays" describes the same object ("you"), as you would in an application letter after university. The same activity referring to different objects shows a pattern

---

[7] Most readers will be familiar with such brainstorming and the various techniques that can be used in group settings. The main rule is to be positive and playful.

about which we can draw conclusions: "Firm A had success when re-training their long-term employees, Firm B had success when retraining all their employees and even Firm C did better after re-training their mid-management". Your conclusion could be that it is a good idea to retrain employees to prepare them for new market standards. These are simple examples that illustrate how to infer (make an inference) in your reasoning.

Make sure that all groups are complete, more or less. Fill in gaps that have become apparent. Wherever you notice that a group is incomplete, define what is missing and assemble new ideas to fill in the gap. Some of your ideas may be lonely still, without a group. Ask yourself how those unaffiliated ideas relate to your general theme and whether they can be connected to a group, or whether you will need to start a new and bigger group for them. You can think of stand-alone ideas as temporary orphans, and your task is to establish and connect them to a broader family that they should be grouped with. At this stage (as in others) you will find yourself using an internal 'mini'-DAGOR procedure to resolve any difficulties that you may run into.

Order these groups into an organizing structure. This is a task of visualization, using either outline format, the pyramid, an argumentative circle, or a mind map.

Your structure should be governed by the principle of writing for the reader. Focus on those arguments or points which are most likely to convince the reader. You should not have more than three to five main points. Additional points will not convince the reader but may begin to bore her. If you describe a process, more than five points are easily forgotten. Eliminate or re-structure accordingly.

Structure this main-idea first: always give the reader an overview before taking her into the details: "Tell them what you'll tell them, tell them, tell them what you told them". In the pyramid, you would be moving from the top down, in the argumentative circle from the centre outward. Arrange the thesis, arguments, subarguments and supports accordingly.

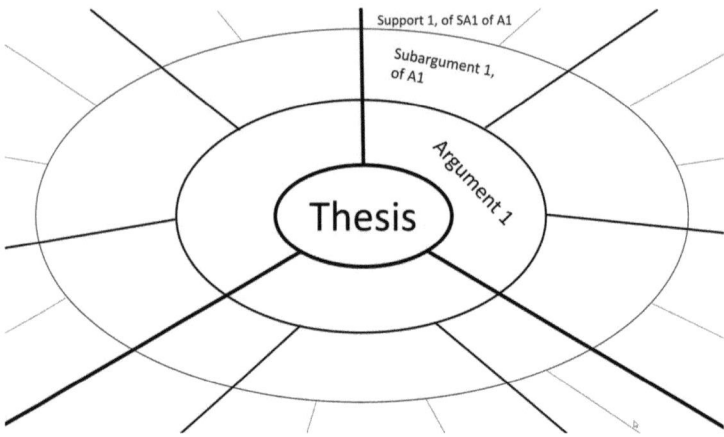

Remember, as described in the section on structures, there are three sensible types of organizing ideas: a chronological process ("first step, second step, etc."), a structural dissection of a system ("legislative, executive, judicative") or a comparative selection ("the three most effective measures to improve customer service in our workplace"). To recall these types helps you to keep the groups coherent.

Reviewing the structure: do this before you start to write. You must have a visual outline, in a form that gets your ideas onto paper, walls, whiteboard or screen, and out of your head, so that you can see it all at once. Now check whether your argument makes sense. Will your paper convince the reader? Do the points cohere and relate directly to the argument on the next level? Does the thesis summarise the arguments, do the arguments summarize the subarguments, and the subarguments the supports? Are the arguments arranged in a sensible order?

You can test your proposed structure by designing your introduction. The classic formula is SCR: Situation,

Complication, Resolution. Say something general and uncontroversial about the topic. Then describe the complication that arises for you, and show how you propose to resolve it. You can turn those three steps around as you see fit (and occasionally, even add a rhetorical fourth -- Q, for question). The three aspects should, however, always be included to clarify to the reader how what you say relates to the context that she is starting from.

How you write this introduction depends on the knowledge level of your reader, and other adjectives you have used to characterize her. You need more context if your average reader knows little. You can get to the point more quickly if your 3-5 characterizing adjectives have highlighted that your intended audience is already well informed.

The process of designing your introduction helps you to review the focus, the coherence and the balance of your arguments. For in developing your introduction, you are forced to articulate your thesis once more -- and to offer it as a resolution to a specific complication. The effect achieved is that of a magnifying glass. If you spot a mistake, go back through the DAGOR procedure. Improve your plan until you are satisfied that it fulfils its purpose and that it is oriented towards the reader.

And only now start to write your document.

- ***Example of DAGOR result***

Here is how you could use DAGOR when putting together a job application. Rather than explaining why everything in your life (including your love of basketball) qualifies you to be the event manager, you do a thorough analysis of what is required in the job description (Define), consider all that you offer (Assemble), analyse and synthesize (Group) and structure (Organize) the information in a visual outline. Having reviewed your plan to check whether it is properly targeted onto the purpose and written for the reader, you can now write as part of your cover letter:

- "In my last position, I was responsible for organising our organization's regional meetings and conferences, two per month, with up to 80 participants from up to nine countries. I thus have experience in co-ordinating complex schedules and in working to tight deadlines and within strict financial constraints."

If you address the reader's main concern, you will demonstrate – rather than simply talk about – how much your previous work experience has indeed qualified you for the position.

- ***Co-operate as much as possible***

In preparing professional documents, solicit your colleagues' input as much as possible. It can make sense to discuss outlines, since it's easier and faster to change them than an entire document. Show other people your drafts and offer to check their drafts. Their advice can increase your impact. As you are writing for someone else anyway, you should not hesitate to show the document or an outline to colleagues or friends.

DAGOR here can be a diagnostic tool, too. Does the proposed document work with the right definition? Has it assembled the appropriate materials? Are those materials grouped and organized coherently? Has the final review smoothened out any remaining edges? What can be improved?

If you are asked to give feedback, provide fair comments. Good criticism is oriented towards results. Identify what works in a text and what, in your opinion, could be improved. Suggest how the writing "could be made even better by [concrete suggestion]". Avoid saying that writing is bad – even relaxed people can become defensive. Complaining about shortcomings offers little guidance on how to move forward.

How would we, for example, constructively criticize someone whose criticism is unconstructive? We could say "your comments would be even more useful if you could explicitly suggest how to address the shortcomings you have identified in the second and third paragraph".

Through co-operation you will develop the skill of giving constructive advice to those with less experience – and your own writing will improve as a result of learning how to identify possible improvements.

- ***Practice and Discipline***

To successfully execute the DAGOR procedure takes practice. First, you need to understand each step of this process. It is precisely the knowledge of how to break the process down into separate steps that will help you do it properly. Each time you follow the steps in the proper sequence, you will get better.

Show discipline. Take it slowly and do DAGOR methodically. Fully complete each step before you continue to the next stage. Most errors are due to a lack of discipline. Do not try to do too many things at once. Ideas, like glasses and plates, fall and shatter if you carry too many at once, without a well-practiced technique.

But also, be disciplined about being undisciplined. In the phase where you are assembling information, everything must be allowed. It has even been said that there are no people who are not creative – just those who are neither patient nor methodical enough to wait until they have generated a suitable idea. If you keep re-arranging material, especially if you discuss it with colleagues, you will usually find a suitable solution.

Is DAGOR the only planning system for writing? Certainly not. You may have alternative ideas, and there are many different ideas on how to plan. You could contract or expand DAGOR to include fewer, or more, steps. The advantage of DAGOR is that we have a sensible number of steps that are easy to remember, and that capture the distinct nature of the activities.

DAGOR helps you to recognize that these steps, at least for some people, can correspond to different moods: focused for the definition, exuberant for the assembly of materials, playful for the grouping, systematic for the organizing of materials, and critical for the final review.

In my experience, successful communicators begin DAGOR with an open mind, to discover and enjoy the planning. Keeping this open mind helps people identify new and potentially neglected aspects (the orphaned ideas mentioned above) that often prove particularly engaging and innovative. Use DAGOR for discovery, and you are most likely to do well.

Specific Applications

How to use these tools in practice.

You now know the four principles, three structures for visualization, two formulas, and a workable procedure. With 4321 these are easy to remember. The following pages will show you how to apply this conceptual framework to documents.

As we discuss the documents, we use the same pattern to make the overall approach as accessible as possible:

- we cover the principles, so that you thoroughly understand the purposes of each document, and the needs of your readers;
- we examine the format of each document, telling you what to include;
- you will be guided through each step of the procedure, making the process easier for you;
- we will tell you anything else you need to know in a sub-section on items you should remember.

This structure reflects the approach you could take when thinking out about any such task, moving from general considerations to specific detail, including a conscious reflection on the process you embark on.

You should, ideally, read the first section on essays even if you do not intend to write them. The reason is that this is a general format for convincing people and once you can write a good essay (and understand how to focus a message) you can write any other document, provided you understand its purpose and format. For this reason, too, essays remain a central tool for testing people's judgement, both in leading universities and in entrance examinations for civil services, around the world.

With the sections on other documents, they are mostly self-contained. You may find it useful to read all of them, to get a better understanding of main formats of professional communication. Students may also find it useful to read some of the sections on other documents, to see how what they learn for writing essays is broadly transferable. Alternatively, read a section when you have a specific task you need to accomplish.

A number of further professional documents are not listed here. But they follow the same principles and you apply the systematic approach outlined above to the specific document you are writing.

Throughout, remember that your thinking and your judgement are required to put the advice into practice.

Documents: Purposes, Audiences, Formats

Essay

A general template for convincing people.

- ## *Purpose – Principle I*

In an essay, you try to convince the reader. Once you succeed in writing good argumentative essays, you will be able to write all other documents described in this book. A good essay demands that you define a clear and specific purpose. It encourages you to write for your reader. And it forces you to state your main idea first – to write clearly and intelligibly by structuring your information hierarchically.

Essays always should be argumentative essays. In such essays, you communicate your conclusion about a specific topic. You tell the reader the result of your hard thinking: you offer your evaluation and explain why you believe it is the best conclusion. You make a statement that can be contradicted. That statement should be potentially vulnerable, otherwise there is nothing to discuss. There is little to contradict in the statement that David Kakabadze was a Georgian painter. However, if I say that Kakabadze was an eminent early modernist painter with profound influence, some fruitful disagreement is possible.

The argumentative essay is the only type of essay that is worth writing. There are, however, two other types of essays that still are being written. These two dinosaurs are the descriptive and the debative essay. Arguably, the main reason these types of pseudo-essays are not yet extinct is that their writers have not yet been introduced to the advantages of writing argumentative essays.

In the descriptive essay, the author describes something in a neutral tone. The writer starts, for example, by saying that the painter David Kakabadze was born in 1889. The writer continues to describe Kakabadze's life, his studies in Petersburg, his time in Paris and so on, ending with his last years before his death in 1952. Now, it is admirable if you can get a parrot to repeat these facts. It is also acceptable for an entry in Wikipedia or in a dictionary and even for an essay written by a young teenager. But it is unsatisfactory as an essay because a recitation of facts does not convince the reader that this listing matters, in that vast universe of facts that we inhabit today. Unless there are factual errors, there is nothing to contradict. For the reader, and for the writer, it is much more engaging if you provide the reader with a debatable statement.

I have before me, as I write, a print of a painting by Kakabadze, "Imereti Landscape", 1915. I could now tell you that it shows a big mountain with different shades of green and yellow, and that there is a river in the middle. That is descriptive.

But if I were to write an essay about that painting, I should think of an argument. What, for example, makes this painting special? My first impression is that Kakabadze successfully combines traditional concerns of portraying landscape with a courageous technique that is modern. His technique shows in broad, fat strokes of his brush. If you look closely, you see just how crude his strokes are, how smudges of dried green and yellow paint form ridges on the canvas. Yet this crudeness defines its success, giving the painting an instability that makes the mountain landscape, including the river, come alive to me.

I hope that this helps you to see the difference between descriptive and argumentative essays. In an argumentative essay the author explains her assessment of a specific issue. Such an assessment is more compelling to read because you encounter an idea that you can object to and engage with.

Organising information around an idea is not only more interesting, it also is a more effective way of communicating. The author has done some thinking for you. She highlights how information could be relevant to you. She creates a question in your mind that will help you to follow the flow of information.

Most descriptive essays can be rewritten to become argumentative essays without much effort – not least because in the descriptive essay some type of argument usually is implied, though not stated accessibly. Rather than describing Kakabadze's life from his birth to his death, you could discuss the specific factors that had a large influence on him. You will probably mention his rural Georgian origin, born close to Khoni, and his contacts with painting and painters abroad, such as Marcel Duchamp, while he lived in Paris from 1919 to 1927. Your thesis could be that Kakabadze shows how painting can be both local and global, shaped by where you come from but also part of – and contributor to – a specific historical moment that extends across much of the world.

When you have to rewrite a descriptive essay, ask yourself why and in what way the subject could be relevant to the reader. The fully developed answer to this question is your thesis: "Kakabadze's work is significant because ..." (give specific reasons). Now the reader gets a clear answer to the question of why he is reading the essay. Restructuring essays through this method can transform a boring paper into a rewarding read. Notice that the method again follows DAGOR. As a first step, you define, or redefine, what is relevant for the reader and then assemble material, and proceed through the next steps.

What about the debative essay? In a debative essay the author takes the reader through a long discussion between different sides. A debative essay is like a conversation between people who disagree. Although such conversations are entertaining in real life or when set out by master novelists, they are mostly dull to read if written in abstract prose. Such a debative style does little more than mimic what the two sides are saying. An advance over the descriptive essay as we now have two parrots to listen to – but we still lack a balanced evaluation from an outsider.

Here, too, the writer refuses to do the work he should do: to take a position and try to convince the reader that this is a strong, or at least a sensible, position to hold.

There are, of course, other types of writing in which such a clear judgement should not be taken. In articles, journalists should explicitly not try to convince you that one solution is right, but rather let you see multiple sides and voices on ongoing events. Moreover, for young pupils at school a debative essay is a good exercise because it helps them to discover that there are different plausible sides to complex issues. But for a fully educated person, it is not a great use of time to write and read such essays. Your author takes you through his thought processes but this is not what you want. When you order food in a restaurant you want a dish to be delivered to your table. You do not want to be taken into the kitchen to participate in the cooking. Similarly in reading, you want a finished product of thinking, not to be a witness to the process of thinking.

The way to turn a debative essay into an argumentative one is that you come to a conclusion about the main idea you want to engage the reader on. You tell the reader from the beginning what this conclusion is. Ideally, you have made a decision about the relative merits of the different sides. But you could also argue that there are two plausible interpretations of Kakabadze's work. Here, too, there is a discernible idea which forces you to work to convince your reader: first, you will argue that only two interpretations are entirely plausible, and stand out in comparison to the rest. Secondly, you will demonstrate why those two interpretations are plausible. If you want to extend the argument further, you may want to show what it means to choose between those two (or however many) interpretations.

If your conclusion is that both sides are broadly right (or wrong), as is the case in many conflicts, you say this at the beginning. Whatever your conclusion, you substantiate the thesis with arguments that are likely to convince the reader.

The main point to remember is that an essay has the purpose of convincing the reader. In practice, this mission makes essays easier to write. In descriptive and debative essays you are never quite sure how much to include. When writing argumentative essays, you have a simple principle: you include whatever you think will convince the reader.

- ### *Writing for the Reader – Principle II*

To write for a reader in an essay primarily means that you make a good and convincing case in which the logical connections between the ideas are solid. You will adapt to your specific readership – how much they know about their topic, their current beliefs and expectations. As you are trying to convince them, you will go out to pick them up, rather than hoping that they will come to your position.

What are the five adjectives that characterize readers of essays? Here is how I often feel, especially when reading student essays: impatient, critical, bored, thirsting for original ideas, relatively knowledgeable (in the fields I read essays in). Let's unpack these sentiments of essay-readers.

To start with, many readers are impatient. We have other things to do, and thus the essay needs to engage, right from the beginning, with its introduction, and then hold our attention through well-reasoned argument, and by keeping the essay on track, without distractions.

Like most readers, I am critical when reading, even if an essay holds my attention. An essay is a claim to authority, and most readers want to see whether that claim is warranted. As readers, we thus look closely on whether we find claims to be logical and persuasive. If we find gaps in the logic, even just with one argument, this may well lead us to be skeptical about the entire claim to authority.

Although many people are naturally curious, even people with an open mind can easily get bored when reading essays, especially when reading one essay after another in a single setting, as you do when grading. By the fourth essay, they begin to blend into one another. Overcooked ratatouille describes the experience of most readers in a university context. Yet even outside university, if you have read on any issue for a few years – democracy, elections, travel, urban development, education, you name the topic – the essays begin to look alike. Democracy is good! Elections matter! Human rights must be protected! Travel educates and refreshes! Urban development should be for people, not for cars! Education is the most important investment in society! Emphasize creativity!

Most people thus are thirsting for original ideas. They want a new angle on familiar issues. You can achieve this originality by applying an established idea to a new and specific context. How does democratic decision-making work in unregulated domains in the Internet, and in local subgroups that previously have not been studied? How have election finance mechanisms worked for small parties, in the last elections? What are the little tricks that allow travelers to invest more into the local economy, and what are the best examples of its application in Georgia? In urban development, what are the measures that get more people onto bicycles? In primary and secondary education, are there proven methods for getting children to increase their ability to persist and concentrate for long stretches of time?

Originality is less likely to be achieved by sticking with the very big ideas, or by taking a facile counter position. Skeptical of democracy and of elections? Plato beat you to that. Not sure about travel? Read Thoreau's Walden. You think cars are the future for all cities? Tunnel diggers agree. Your readers likely will have seen the well-worn opposite points of view, too. Go particular, to the details, or into crossovers, and you are most likely to engage your audience.

Though people often read on issues they already are knowledgeable in, such focus can provide a refreshing angle, to make even the 27th essay engaging. The text should still be accessible to relative newcomers, for example by briefly summarizing a definition, but an essay is not an extended explanation, nor a Wikipedia article. An essay succeeds when even people that are steeped in the field can take something fresh from reading it.

The five adjectives I have described are the sentiments that I bring to reading essays. Find out what your audience cares about, and what is important to them when they read your writing.

More generally with essays, a usual requirement of writing for the reader is that you will cite your sources. As an essay is the expression of your own personal judgement, the reader wants to know how your views stand in relation to an established debate in the field. Some younger students are worried about citing their source because they think that they will look less original. That concern is misplaced. Putting the ideas of others together in new ways is an act of creation, and at its best even of originality.

Get your relationship with your sources right: although you want to cite sources that back up your arguments, and that are credible and respected in the field, you should not be dominated by them. You are in charge and have the authority. The spotlight is on you, and on your writing. Writing an essay is not an exercise of reverence where exclaiming the names of magical authority will make your troubles go away.

The main point of citations is proper identification. You give the reader the possibility to verify your citation and to follow it up in case she gets interested in that idea. In general, you should give all the information that the reader needs to identify the source. Put the most important information first: Author, Title, Publishing Firm, Location, Year, page number(s). For journals or newspapers, you again give the information that the reader needs to find the source herself. When citing web sites, you should note the date when the information was retrieved from the Internet. If the links are too long to cite sensibly, consider using one of the many link shorteners that are available on the Internet.

Yet the precise format of a citation varies. Institutions and academic fields often require a specific style. These styles are quick to find and simple to follow. Conforming to this style shows that you are aware and ready to adopt the discipline's habits. As many people have remarked, such styles are a little like tribal ceremonies, often impractical yet powerful celebrations of membership. For these tribal reasons, you may want to comply with conventions. Focus your energies on engaging with substantive issues, rather than formatting battles.

- *Main idea first – Principle III*

As we noted above, putting your main idea first makes your paper more interesting to read. It makes the paper more honest, too: you present your ideas in such a way that the reader can clearly identify them from the beginning. The reader knows what you want to convince her about. Make an attractive case, yet hide nothing and don't attempt to manipulate the reader. While you may hoodwink some readers, those that notice that you are trying to manipulate them will no longer trust you, being extremely sceptical of anything you write in the future. Conversely, even those that disagree with you will appreciate if you clearly present your idea in such a way that they find it easy to identify their disagreement.

For your idea to be plausible, it should be specific, as highlighted above. Most papers fail because they are too general. Students try to address many themes at once ("The Future of Georgian Foreign Policy"). They say little about a lot, rather than saying a lot about focused issues that matter. Essays, like buildings or bridges, collapse if you are too ambitious with too little material.

How, then, can we successfully focus a topic? Take the example of writing about Georgian culture. Obviously, this is too general. Focus on architecture? Still far too broad. But you could concentrate on forms in Georgian architecture. And you could then develop the thesis that a key theme in Georgian architecture is an endless re-interpretation of how the square and the circle interact. As it turns out, this is an idea that Kakabadze put forward in a film in the late 1920s. He saw the origin of these themes in Georgian architecture in the Darbazi, houses built on square foundations with a round fireplace in the middle. He illustrated his argument by concentrating on one building, the Basilica in Bolnisi, making a powerful case by focusing on a single building.

Defining your specific topic and developing a thesis from this takes some practice. Unfortunately, many people leave university without having learnt this skill. They thus miss out on a technique that is key for success in communication.

In the first section of this book, we already mentioned one technique for focusing: to write your introduction with SCR. In this part a table shows how you can turn your interest in a field into a specific topic. You succeed by focusing on smaller details, ideally those that are representative of the whole.

If you are struggling to specify, the action formula helps you narrow down your topic. Take a general theme and ask: who? What? When? How? Where? Why? Interrogate your theme, and you will move towards articulating a manageable specific topic.

Once you have studied the table and have practiced turning a few general topics into specific theses, you have made great progress. Try this with fellow students, friends or family. Wacky ideas can make this exercise engaging.

General [what]
National tradition

Broad [when]
National tradition nowadays

Specific topic [who]
National dresses that many of us sometimes wear

Thesis [where]
"In Georgia, all people should be obliged to wear national dress from Wednesday to Sunday."

Potential arguments could be:

1.) People wearing national dress would make Georgia more attractive to itself, and promote a sense of unity and dignity.
2.) More national dress would make Georgia more attractive to tourists, and thus improve the economy.
3.) People wearing more national dress would increase the demand for clothing that is locally produced, and thus help the local garment industry.
4.) People not wanting to wear national dress from Wednesday to Sunday could pay for an exemption, which could fund social programs.

In this case, we have not even exhausted the action formula, because you could be asking *how* exactly we will implement the law. As mentioned, it helps if the topic is absurd, as this gives you permission to play. Concrete applied topics ("how to improve primary education") can be more difficult for practice because require expert knowledge and often are fraught with unintended consequences. You want topics that allow you to play around, and which give you a sense of discovery.

Note here and when looking at the table that what is general and broad depends on the perspective. If you are a specialist in Georgian family law, what seems like a "specific topic" to us non-specialists may still appear "broad" or even "general" to you. The rule is to work until you have narrowed down the general theme into a topic that seems relevant to your audience and manageable for you.

DAGOR here is particularly useful, because in the first step of defining you have significant opportunity to narrow down your topic, and focus on a manageable topic.

The table below gives examples of how you turn a general field into a specific topic. You can also see how a thesis relates to such a topic – of course many alternative theses are possible. Note how the arguments directly support the thesis, and how specification follows the action formula.

"Field"	General	Broad	Specific topic	Thesis	(Potential) arguments
Education	University Education	Skills in university education	The skill of evaluative judgement in university education today	"Evaluative judgement (EJ) is the key skill to be learnt at university now."	1.) EJ is needed to utilize specialized knowledge. 2.) EJ is a skill you keep even while knowledge is forgotten. 3.) EJ is needed in professional, political and private life in a democracy and dynamic market economy.
Ukraine	Ukraine's economy	Problems of the Ukrainian economy	Taxation system is a key factor in Ukraine's economic problems	"Ukraine's poor tax system was a key factor in preventing the development of the Ukrainian economy, before 2014."	1.) Poor tax system forced entrepreneurs to hide assets and profits, making access to credit difficult. 2.) Poor tax system discouraged people from keeping money in the bank. 3.) Poor tax system reduced state income and thereby encouraged corruption.
Georgian literature	Georgian poetry	Georgian poetry as a reflection of politics	Georgian poetry as a reflection of politics prior to independence	"Although only in subtle ways, Georgian pre-independence poetry reflects the instability of the Soviet system."	1.) Georgian pre-indep. poetry reflects the disintegration of trust in the political system. 2.) Georgian pre-indep. poetry begins to name the problems in society. 3.) Georgian pre-indep. poetry starts to express an interest in specifically Georgian themes.
Me	My skills	My management skills	My experience in managing a marketing office in Kyiv	"Having managed a marketing office in Ukraine for two years, I believe I am qualified for the position you offer."	1.) Through my experience, I have learnt to manage tight deadlines. 2.) Through my experience, I have learnt to run internal office organisation, including filing systems. 3.) Through my experience, I know how to manage small-sized financial accounts.

- *Typical Format*

The typical format for a good essay is between 1500-2000 words, a text that can be read in about ten minutes. With this you can pack 9-12 distinct ideas into the essay, at various levels, allowing for a nuanced consideration of a complicated issue. For readers, this length is ideal, as it is long enough to explain complex ideas and short enough to keep the reader engaged. Papers that contain more than 3000 words are less attractive, as they take longer to read. As the thesis and the main arguments remain the same in longer papers, their additional length means additional detail, rather than adding transformative ideas. For the purposes of communicating essential ideas (and of training students to write) this detail is not necessary and can even be a distraction from much-needed focus.

For university purposes, the short paper is suitable, too, because it is complex in its architecture (9-12 ideas need to be arranged), the emphasis is on quality of planning and not on quantity of words. The shortness of the essay forces the students to choose what is important and what should be left aside (a productive learning experience because it is painful), and it is a fairly quick read for the lecturer or fellow students, who have many other concerns that compete for their attention. In exams, 45-60 minutes per essay question have proven to be a good time, especially if there are four (or in the case of 60 minutes three) questions that students must answer.

Yet the format can be scaled up or down. The essay format can be used for documents that summarize main arguments on a single page, in tight prose. Conversely, the essay format can be expanded to become a longer academic paper or even a book. At their best, such books are organized to promote a few powerful ideas that change the way we look at an issue – and they tell us from the beginning what they are trying to do, rather than hiding the revelation until the end.

The overall structure of the essay is simple. The structure can be summarized, as mentioned above, as "tell them what you will tell them, tell them, tell them what you told them". That is: state clearly what you are trying to achieve with your essay, make your arguments and then review what you have said at the end. The structure typically looks like this:

>Introduction and Thesis
>Argument 1
>>Subargument 1
>>>Support 1
>>>Support 2
>>>Support N.
>>Subargument 2...
>>Subargument N...
>Argument 2...
>Argument 3...
>[Further Arguments]
>Conclusion.

The thesis, of course, is a summary of the three arguments, much as the arguments are a summary of the subarguments, and so on. That they are summaries is easy to check: make sure that the wording of the next higher level is repeated. The box below shows you how this is done and how the structure of your essay could look. The emphasis in the example is on the structure of outline, not so much on the content of the argument. The repetitive wording here is extreme, purposefully as a tool to streamline the structure.

Essay Outline on "Benefits of DAGOR"

Introduction:
Situation: the ability to evaluate, i.e. to make balanced judgements, is crucial to success in a market economy and

democracy, as these put emphasis on citizens' independent thinking.

Complication: this crucial skill is not easy to acquire and not taught systematically.

Resolution/Thesis: students can improve their ability to evaluate by writing argumentative essays using the DAGOR method

Arguments

1.) Evaluation is required to Define the task:

(i.) To define the task you have to analyse the purpose and audience

(ii.)To define the task you have to identify the scope of the project.

(iii.)   To define the task you have to choose which theme is worth tackling, and then focus it narrowly.

2.) Evaluation is required to Assemble the material:

(i.) To assemble the material you need to decide where to look.

(ii.) To assemble the material you need to decide how deep to look.

(iii.)   To assemble the material you need to decide what is relevant.

3.) Evaluation needs to be applied to Group, Order and Review your ideas:

(i.) To group the material you need to analyse and decide on similarity, difference and connection.

(ii.) To organize the material you need to synthesize and decide what is more and what is less important.

(iii.)   To review you need to go through Situation, Complication and Resolution and decide whether they fit your purpose.

Conclusion

-      Develop the writing of argumentative essays in schools and universities.

-      Teach pupils and students how to use DAGOR

In the conclusion, as you see, nothing new is added. Instead the conclusion summarises the overall paper and takes up ideas that the reader has engaged with while reading this paper. Depending on whom the essay is written for – write for the reader – it may also include an additional appeal to action. If for university officials, the essay would suggest that DAGOR should be introduced and one or two sentences on how staff could be trained to teach this system. Written for students, it would suggest to them how they could begin using DAGOR. In both cases, however, such an additional appeal would have to be brief, like a zooming out from a setting at the end of a movie. The end-section is not where we add major information.

Incidentally, the dissection of structure in the table is a useful tool for analysis. If you are trying to understand what someone else is trying to say, you can break down their arguments into such an outline (or another visualization, as discussed in the first section). The breakdown will allow you to look at the arguments and subarguments and to examine whether they are substantial and make sense.

I have heard an editor of an international news outlet remark that what made one of her (Caucasus-based) journalists particularly good is that she had taken the time to dissect several New York Times articles, by breaking them down in detail. Studying such breakdowns, so the editor, had taught this young journalist how to develop the structure of her own articles.

- *Procedure*

DAGOR can guide you through developing a good paper to the point where you have a complete plan. What you absolutely need to know, however, is that the actual procedure is always a bit chaotic and stressful. DAGOR does not eliminate the chaos – but it gives it a structure that produces good results.

DAGOR has been used to put this guide together. I planned each section with pencil and paper before sitting down to type. To write just this section on essays, I filled 18 pages with hand-written notes. It took quite some time to develop the plan which served as the basis for this section. The writing, then, was much quicker, and required less editing.

With most complex documents, you will go through DAGOR several times. You will produce a rough plan in the beginning, go out and get information and then refine your plan, possibly even change it. Fine-tuning this plan every day helps you to develop your ideas. Some successful companies teach their employees to develop a first-day-hypothesis, an initial tentative thesis that they keep testing against all further information that they assemble. If necessary, they modify or change the hypothesis, day-by-day. They create what we probably could call a cumulative outline. Enriching a structure over time is a very efficient way of capturing and developing ideas.

Throughout, however, the steps remain the same, because you always need to define the specific question you face, get all the relevant information and then process the information by grouping and ordering it. You should also review your results in the end to guard against errors.

You will almost always have new ideas while writing. You need to integrate these into your plan before you begin to write them into your text. Check to see whether the new idea fits into the overall structure – and where it fits best. While building a house, you don't one morning extend one wall because your cousin just gave you an additional 300 bricks. You go back to the architect's plans and carefully integrate any idea before you proceed to change the structure. Similarly in writing, don't keep typing away on an idea that has come into your mind, tempting as that may be. Stream-of-consciousness writing usually goes all over the place, and is easy to spot for the reader. If your new idea is good, it can be integrated into a modified plan.

As we have discussed DAGOR above, here only a summary specific to the essay.

Define the question
Make the question specific, so that the essay has a focused purpose. See above on how to do this. Develop an initial area of interest, and maybe even a rough thesis.

Assemble
Here you try to get ideas and information from any source.

You are the first source. Write up anything that comes into your mind. Do not worry about the order. Just write down the ideas as they come, as many as possible for at least 10 minutes. Do not discard ANY idea at this point, as crazy as the idea at first may appear to you. Further develop your initial question and the rough thesis you started with. Then start your research to answer this question and to see whether your thesis can be substantiated.

Use whatever helps you: Internet searches, books, journals, your own research including conversations and interviews, or a hook such as a quote or striking statistic. Decide how deep you want to research the theme. For a serious paper, you should take at least a few days. Keep taking notes, short summaries of the information that has turned out to be relevant.

Be orderly. Write the date and the subject on the pages that you fill with your notes. When you quickly assemble information on a single sheet, remember to write numbers in front of each item, to speed up the procedure that follows.

Group
The ideas need to be grouped. Which of these ideas belong together? Do they refer to the same object or to the same activity? Then they may belong in the same group.

Write down the groupings on a new sheet, even if this is just by noting down the number of each item that you had assembled.

It is an excellent idea to turn off the Internet and put the phone aside while you work on grouping and organizing. This part of the DAGOR process is so difficult that you will feel an urge to do something else, like checking e-mail or your favourite social network. I often switch my computer to airplane mode, to free myself of distraction.

Order

Analyse how the ideas in the group relate to each other: are they on the same level? Is there any idea which summarises the others? Is there any idea which does not belong? At this point, you may start discarding ideas. Below, you see a box in which there are four groups. In every group, there is one idea that does not belong, and one that summarises the ideas that do belong. The ordering you do with the box is a simplified example of what you should be doing when writing your essay. The examples are radically simplified, for illustration. The clear thinking in such groupings and categories is a key feature of quality analysis – and the more specialized and abstract the terms, the closer one does need to look, as the box illustrates.

1.	Cats	1.	Tomato
2.	Dogs	2.	Vegetables
3.	Children	3.	Sulguni cheese
4.	Animals	4.	Carrots
1.	Value-added tax	1.	Free and fair elections
2.	Tobacco tax	2.	Marxism
3.	Sources of state revenue	3.	Fascism
4.	Profit tax exemption	4.	Political ideologies
5.	Income tax	5.	Maoism

The relevant summaries depend, of course, on the specific context. When you say "things I like", you may list free and fair elections, tomato, sulguni cheese, dogs and children – in almost all other contexts such a group would not make much sense.

After assigning a theme to each group, develop a structure of thesis, arguments, subarguments, supports. Create a visualization (outline, argumentative circle, pyramid, mind map), that helps you to see the bigger picture.

Balance out the arguments: costs versus benefits, advantages versus disadvantages. Only state counter-arguments implicitly. For example:

- "Although the water is very cold, a short swim close to the shore will re-invigorate you."

is better than:

- "Should we swim in the water? After all it is very cold and this may have a number of harmful effects. Also, when we swim very far into the lake, it may become dangerous. But then we don't have to swim out very far, nor stay in very long. And the advantage that it will reinvigorate us is more important."

A parade of contradictory arguments is irritating to readers because they do not know where you are trying to take them.

Other examples of implicit inclusion of counter-arguments: "although imposing additional cost, this investment should increase our earnings by X% within three months." Or: "Although initially requiring extra effort, putting advice and support for small- to medium-sized farmers online will help to expand hazelnut production, as much more farmers can be reached at lower cost." And so on: you should now be able to formulate such statements yourself.

Review

This is the process of checking whether you got everything right. Write up your planned structure neatly, either in an outline or in one of the visualizations. Read it a few times, taking breaks in between, to check whether the structure is plausible. The first plan rarely is right. Keep changing it – going back through DAGOR if necessary – until it is coherent. At this point, you can begin to plan your introduction.

- *Remember: Plan, Third Principle, Collect*

An essay never is better than its plan. A plan is easier to change than an essay. Keep working on the plan until it is right. Co-operate with others, to improve the plan.

Keep to the third principle, of main-idea first. Everything will flow from the main idea, and refining this into a nuanced and focused thesis is your biggest challenge. In a next step, the same principle applies on the lower levels as well, for every argument and every paragraph. Every paragraph should start with a clear declarative statement, a so-called topic sentence, and further sentences must develop the idea from this first sentence. You should only deviate from this principle if you know that it helps the reader, as a very conscious decision. Otherwise stay with the standard structure for your paragraphs, such as "declaration, explanation, example". Whenever you are stuck, go back up to the next higher level, and connect your writing to what you were trying to convey, overall.

Writing argumentative essays always involves uncomfortable uncertainty, while you try to figure out how to structure your ideas. This discomfort is normal and even healthy. The nervousness indicates that your mind is alert and continuously checking for mistakes. The best thing is to tolerate the uncertainty and make your life comfortable otherwise (by taking more frequent breaks in difficult moments). Be patient. Do avoid the typical beginner's mistake: holding on to the first idea to escape this emotional challenge.

Experienced writers can, of course, write excellent essays in a less hierarchically structured style than the one described in this section. You can read essays that seem to flow naturally from idea to idea in the weekly *New Yorker* magazine, for example, which has some of the best writing in English. But I have never seen a beginner succeed in writing good essays with similar dramatic composition because what seems effortless is difficult. The easy grace rests on many years of strenuous practice. The individual pieces of writing are constructed over days, weeks and sometimes months. To move in such a direction, you should first teach yourself to write a tightly structured argumentative essay before you attempt to write in any other style. As with music, you must excel at the exercises before you try the full piano concerto.

For teaching purposes, students should hand in outlines together with essays, or even before they hand in the essay. This visual outline should be neat and readable. The outline allows the teacher to quickly identify structural shortcomings – otherwise the teacher needs to break down the essay into an outline to give a proper diagnosis. By saving the teacher time, this practice leaves more time for constructive suggestions. The outline itself can serve as a basis for discussion or of suggesting what could be improved. Moreover, the submission of the outline ensures that students understand that they need to complete an outline, and reduces the temptation to just type away on a computer without a plan.

If you see good essays, collect them in a folder and look at them from time to time to find out why they are successful and to check how your own view of these essays has developed, as you get better and better at writing.

Memo

A template for professional communication with colleagues, superiors or subordinates. You can use it to convince them (i.e. to get them to act) or to describe something to them that they may need to know to make their own judgements.

- ### *Purpose: Get Colleagues to Act – Principle I*

The memo is the practical cousin of the essay. The purpose of the memo is internal communication within an organization. The memo is more direct and less formal than external communication. Within your organization, everybody will work (roughly) towards the same purpose. The communication is more practical, as the overall goal is given. You will find it easy to write a good memo if you can write a good argumentative essay.

The main task in a memo is to clearly define the purpose you have. What was written in the first section of this book directly applies. You should have a visual image of what you are trying to achieve by writing your memo. This image should become precise enough to answer to the action formula: who does what how when where why?

Some action should be the result of your memo. At the very least, your colleagues should ask themselves: does this matter to me? What do I need to do to adapt to this new information? If you are entirely sure that there is nothing whatsoever for them to do, then the memo probably should not be circulated to these colleagues.

When writing a memo on skills deficiencies, for example, you may want your boss to agree that the staff needs training to improve their handling of the booking system. You thus have the image that your boss will invite a qualified trainer. And with the image you have the next question: who will be the trainer and what kind of training will it be? When? Where?

Similarly, I have been drafting this book with an image of you in mind. I imagine you initially reading this at home and then picking it up again in the office when trying to write a document. Primarily, I see you thinking a lot with a pencil in your hand and taking notes *before* you start writing. *How* are you preparing to write in the image in my mind? By making your decisions according to the principles, by using the formulas to fill the templates with your ideas. (Additionally, I created a checklist because when visualizing, I imagined you may find a worksheet useful when sitting at your desk.) And *why* are you making an effort? Because you want to do better and perhaps also because you share the belief that any country's development depends on the professional ability of its citizens. If citizens can communicate professionally, they can coordinate, agree, achieve efficiency and do things together that would be impossible to do by oneself.

- *Busy, Skeptical, Nervous, Action-Oriented Readers - II Principle*

Tell the reader which action you suggest. Give them the information that they need to react. Put yourself in their position and ask: what do I want to know? If they dislike certain actions that you will propose, spend more time explaining why these measures are needed. Adapt the content of the memo specifically to their knowledge. You can use the standard form for introductions (Situation, Complication, Resolution) if this is a longer memo.

If proposing a course of action, explain why you think that this proposal is good as you would in an essay (on this topic see the section on Policy/Project Proposal). Be short and concise. Eliminate any potential for misunderstanding.

Gear the writing to your reader's position in the organization. Proposals to a superior need to consider all their concerns. Here are the questions that I typically have when I read a memo:

1. Does this proposed activity solve the problem, and does it *actually* solve the problem? In other words, superiors want to be convinced that everyone and everything has been thought about. Will all those who will be affected agree with the idea? Are there any unintended consequences that may arise from the proposed idea? Are the risks covered? Ideally, I want to see that the proposed measure already works somewhere else, and can be scaled up, or sensibly transferred to what our organization does.

2. How is the proposed action aligned with the strategic priorities? Does it contribute to solve a problem we actually need to solve? In any organization, there are dozens of things you could do at any moment, but should not focus on. In one organization I was running, I received a memo on creating a new logo and visual design for the organization, a few weeks after arriving, and about three years after the organization launched. The organization's logo was not amazing, but it was perfectly functional, and we had lots of other things to. I told my colleague we needed to focus on urgent problems. We kept the logo for another six years, and had a good string of successes with the existing visual design, for all its limitations. In other words, make sure you fully understand both the stated and the unstated strategic priorities your bosses are working towards.

3. What are the numbers, on any detail? For any item that is measurable, what is the measure? Primarily, I want to see the costs that derive from the proposed actions, in financial terms. If we are to bring in the trainer, what would that cost? Provide numbers on what is often

called the "level of effort", i.e. staff time. As a manager, you do not want to agree to Luka undertaking additional market research outside the office that you thought would take one afternoon, and now he has disappeared for three weeks, claiming that he is doing a special project for you, as you had agreed to his memo. Luka should therefore specify in the memo how long that additional market research will take. Any substantive issue in the memo should be described in numbers, such as problems, delays or additional costs. If we have a $300 problem, we do not want to spend $3000 on (maybe) solving it.

4. Does this memo potentially annoy or insult anyone? Less experienced writers can easily overlook that what they write can be misconstrued, or end up in the wrong hands. Part of the challenge is structural. When you propose a solution, you often have to highlight a problem, and a careless wording can suggest that a particular person is the problem. Similarly, some people (or departments) may think of themselves as the solution, and may resent that they have been passed over. Managers want a memo to solve one problem, not to create several new ones. By listening to your colleagues, and how they have been burned, you learn much about the sensitivities.

5. Lastly, next steps. What is the next action that is needed to move this issue forward? If there are alternatives, how do we evaluate them? Who is needed, and what level of permission is needed, from whom? Do not forget the little things, for example talking to people in procurement how a particular service can be obtained – and then checking with others whether your interlocutor in procurement can be trusted. Especially in large organizations, little things can easily trip you up. In one organization, we wanted to tender out a service, and the

procurement person had forgotten that under WTO rules, tenders over $500,000 needed to be put on a special system. The entire tender was derailed, the project delayed by months, demoralizing the team. Figure out the way ahead for your bosses, and help them avoid such pitfalls, primarily by building good relations with everyone across an organization, and making sure that you understand whether they are experienced enough to give you competent advice. If they have not done something before, be sceptical if they claim it can easily be done, and develop alternative plans.

More immediately, though, highlight the two or three steps that can be taken (using the action formula: who does what how when where why?) upon reading the memo.

Summarizing the concerns above, these five adjectives come to mind: sceptical; prioritizing strategy; emphasis on diplomacy/avoiding internal conflict; quantitative, especially with cost; next-action-oriented.

Those five concerns are not an exhaustive list, but they easily cover 80% of the concerns on my mind as I read a memo. They are natural concerns for managers to have, and most likely people you are working for share at least some of them. How to find out? Ask them what items they would like to be covered.

Some managers have very specific ideas. One manager I once came across, a man who oversaw the development of many standard-setting power tools, wanted any memo to answer two questions, directly: what benefit does this idea bring to our client? What benefit does it bring to us? That was it.

Other managers may not immediately have an articulate answer, but your question can help stimulate a discussion and clarification, and ensure that you know your audience's precise preferences, to further focus your writing.

You are, however, not only communicating to your managers, but also to subordinates. When communicating with sub-ordinates, remain polite and try to convince your sub-ordinates that what you propose makes sense for them. Organizations run well if their members believe in their mission and you will get support if you keep convincing your fellow workers that what you are doing together makes sense. Share concrete examples of impact that is credible, ideally from an outside source, to motivate. Potentially integrate such validation into your memo, when for some reason you ask your team to make an extra effort.

In addition, you will need to write memos to communicate horizontally within your organization. Information needs to be exchanged among colleagues, not only travel up and down the hierarchy. Participants in seminars regularly mention that they think there is not enough sideways communication, so that they repeatedly find themselves surprised by events in their own organization. As a manager, you can contribute to improving horizontal communication by setting clear rules, and by designating one person who is the main point of contact on an issue, or an outside relationship, who keeps an overview and should be informed on all events.

Other than keeping the person responsible (issue, project, external relationship, geographic area) informed, there are no hard rules on how – and how often -- horizontal information is to be shared. Ask your counterparts what they prefer: always being copied; receiving a daily, weekly or monthly update; or only being contacted once particular issues/milestones/problems or people are involved. Discussing what-if scenarios can help to structure these discussions, and clarify how you can best contribute to successful coordination in your organization.

- ### *Main Idea First: What to Do*

It is vital that in a memo you state the main idea first. Say what you expect (or suggest) the reader to do. They are busy with many other items and will often read your memo in a hurry. You must not bury a crucial piece of information somewhere in the document, accidentally or on purpose. Draft the memo to ensure that key information is upfront and easily accessible.

Structure the memo as you would any longer text, if there are several ideas. The techniques for structuring explained in the first part of the book, and those for structuring an essay directly apply.

Make the important information stand out visually, with sub-headings or bold letters. Ensure that the entire memo is as easy to read as possible.

- ### *Typical format*

Memos have a standard format. The header tells whom they are written for, whom they are from, when they were created and what they are about. Roughly these items correspond to the header of e-mails (to, from, date, re). The memo should include where you can be reached, and potentially if you will be away on travel, in the period while the memo is discussed.

The subsequent page should repeat, at least, the date of the memo and its subject. Proper identification helps people to keep their material in order. You can put this information in the header or footer of the document. Every memo that has more than one page needs page numbers.

In the subject line, you must state precisely what the memo is about. This line should be tightly focused so that the reader immediately understands what you want.

For focussing, apply the procedure we used to define the specific topic in the essay. To give an example:

General: Internal communication

Broad: Improving internal communication

Specific topic: Improving the precision of E-mail subject lines

Thesis: "All staff are asked to write precise E-mail subject lines, stating the precise issue, and what action is required, when corresponding internally and externally, including critical dates or numbers where appropriate, from now on. This rule is being established to improve the flow and accuracy of communication for the ministry."

See how the "thesis" follows the action formula. Only "where" is omitted because it is clear that it refers to staff looking at their screens. Again, the example is for illustrative purposes. Details and tone could vary. Staying with the example, here is how the memo could be phrased to convince staff, by adopting the introduction formula.

Situation:
- "E-mail is the main tool the ministry uses for internal communication, and as such the efficient e-mail communication can help the ministry to work well, coordinate its activities, to maximize the ministry's impact."

Complication:
- "Recently, however, it has become clear that in many respects, current e-mail use is not as effective as it could be. A recent audit in the ministry found that only 45% of examined e-mails were as precise as they could be, giving clear and actionable information. The same audit

found that only 27% of e-mails had a precise and focused subject line, that allows the recipient to understand the content of the e-mail. There thus is considerable room for improvement, in how e-mails are written."

Resolution:

- "As part of our general effort to improve internal communication, we ask all staff to increase the precision of their e-mail communication, starting with accurate E-mail subject lines, stating the precise issue, and what action is required, when corresponding internally and externally, including critical dates or numbers where appropriate, from now on. A short training video by the Training Academy is available below. Department heads are responsible for implementing this change for their teams. We will undertake another audit, in two months, to measure improvements across the ministry. To watch the instructional video, go [here you would insert link/Principle 1, the item you want them to watch]"

Note that we have deviated from telling the staff the main idea first, because we wanted to start with an observation they agree on, following the introduction formula. In a full version, you may want to give a bit more context, and we have deviated slightly from the action formula, in the Resolution. The example nevertheless illustrates how you can structure a memo, to be easily accessible.

If you are looking for an exercise, draft a memo requesting staff to limit their use of social media at the workplace, both on office computers and on private phones. In any such memo, bear in mind that most staff – write for the reader – probably are behaving well and that your communication should reinforce this good behaviour, not alienate people that are being reasonable.

As may have become clear, memos nowadays often are detailed e-mails, that have a formal and binding character. If for some reason the formal nature needs to be emphasized, consider sending the memo as an attached document, with signature. (You can still copy the text into the e-mail, for the convenience of readers that may be reading the item on the mobile device.) If the memo could go outside your own department, you should note your position and department, so that it can be traced to you, and a formal footer should be included. Readers of a memo can, if they think it necessary, pass on your memo to whoever else should be informed. When passing on a hardcopy, it can be initialled by the person who read it, and comments can be written on the margin. (Some established bureaucracies have detailed rules, with different levels of authority commenting with pens of different colours – less practical nowadays, when much information is passed on electronically.)

- *Remember: Procedure, Chains, Adapt to Practice*

The procedure is the same as that for the essay. The one difference is that you define the purpose by thinking of an action formula.

Send memos within the chain of responsibility. Staying within these established channels should be obvious, and yet people still sometimes disregard this iron rule. The biggest culprits here tend to be managers giving instruction downward, outside the chain of management, potentially giving mid-management the feeling that they are left out. Yet the reverse also happens, with people sending memos to the director of the organization, or to another manager who is several levels up, without informing their direct superior first. Just don't ever do that. Your manager will need to reassert control, to show that they are in charge. In reasserting authority, overreaction is normal, often leading to a nasty outcome. Try to manage your managers, rather than bypassing them.

One exception is if behaviour in your department or unit is downright illegal. You may then have a legal obligation to act and notify. Yet such whistleblowing is perilous. Whistle-blowers, even in countries with solid legal frameworks and formal protection mechanisms for whistle-blowers, often end up ostracized and struggle to afterwards find a new job. If you find yourself confronted with extensive illegal or criminal behaviour in the workplace, try to find an experienced outside advisor, someone with more than 15 years of work experience (they should have been through long cycles of ups and downs) and ideally who is familiar with such situations. Do not rely on the advice of friends, as likely they will be out of their depth, for example not understanding the legal risks you run by not reporting, or by reporting in the wrong way. (I am adding this paragraph since I have seen several cases where such whistleblowing went wrong, for the whistle-blower.)

Occasionally, or for special projects, a direct contact beyond the established channels is possible, but contacts across several levels of authority should be treated as a temporary exception, with an awareness that mid-managers normally control vertical lines of communication.

In terms of all memo writing, check what established practice is in your organization, or in comparable organizations. Ask your manager for some samples of memos they liked. Good practice will probably overlap significantly with the suggestions in this section. As a further example of a well-structured memo, look at the Memo to Nino from Paata on the proposal for hiring an assistant for future pitches. As an exercise, devise the header for this memo.

As memos are internal documents, they can be more relaxed in tone, especially if you are communicating with colleagues. Remember, however, that they are open material and may be circulated further. Write in such a way that you would not be embarrassed if the memo is shown to the director of your organization or people outside, such as clients ("this idiot from Guria who keeps paying us too much") or journalists. In public organizations, documents may be subject to Freedom of Information laws (FOIA, in the US context) requests, meaning that your organization may need to release memos and documents, if they are not particularly marked as secret. If you write for the reader, as described above, your memo most likely should be fine, and practice will make you better.

CV

A document with which you are trying to convince employers that you may be useful for them.

- **Purpose: Get Invited, Reference for Interview – Principle I**

The main purpose of a CV usually is to get you an invitation to an interview. In that way, the CV is like an argumentative essay. You are trying to convince your reader of your thesis: "I am the right person for the job because I [meet your three requirements]." The CV has as its arguments the items on your biography. The difference is, of course, that the thesis is not stated and that the CV is not explicitly argumentative. Yet you greatly help yourself in writing your CV when you think of it as the outline of an essay.

A second purpose of the CV is to serve as a point of reference for the interview. Your interviewers will test the positive first impression they had from the CV by checking how solid your arguments are.

Understanding that the CV has an argumentative structure that will be tested will help you to put a compelling CV together. In visualizing the intended result, we can picture people putting your CV aside, positively impressed, to invite you to an interview, and in a second step examining your CV to identify what questions to ask you, so that you can demonstrate your strengths for the position.

- **Motivated, Inquisitive, Attentive, Dismissive Readers – Principle II**

How can we characterize the typical reader of a CV? In many cases, readers may well be: very motivated; inquisitive and even inquisitorial; attentive to detail; dismissive and overwhelmed;

politically or personally motivated, at least sometimes. These adjectives describe my own experience of hiring. Adapt as needed to your likely reader, based on your research, though likely several of the traits will be similar.

Your reader will be highly motivated. They want to find the best employee for the job, and who they hire is perhaps the most important decision they make in their organization. With the right people, even flawed strategies can succeed, as a good team often adapts to circumstance. Conversely, the best strategy cannot succeed without the right people.

Employers typically are looking for commitment and competence, qualities that are needed in combination. Commitment means that you finish what you started. It is a virtue that needs to be practiced and includes taking on challenges and persisting even though the task may turn out to be difficult. Next to professional achievements, commitment can be demonstrated through educational success or sustained voluntary engagement for good causes.

Competence usually means the ability to make balanced judgements (to evaluate) in your field and to put your decision into practice. Judgment is the essence of most jobs. A qualified lawyer must decide what the legal possibilities are. Within his field of expertise, an agronomist must evaluate which fertilizers are suitable in what soil. A construction engineer must judge how much weight can be put on foundations. And even a carpenter should make sensible decisions about what wood to use on a balcony. The ability to make balanced judgements is what your education is about.

Employers will be motivated to see your judgement demonstrated to them, through a listing of your professional achievements. In addition to these professional achievements, you can further demonstrate your judgment, for example by writing on relevant issues, and publishing in recognized outlets, such as a business paper or other relevant publications.

The readers will be inquisitive, when assessing your CV. They will test, in their own mind, whether your claims are convincing. Is the thesis (in its shortest form: "hire me") supported by the arguments (the items on your CV, illustrating competence and commitment). You want to present plausible and detailed arguments, that support your thesis, along the lines of "I have organizing experience through a.) office-management in a marketing company with 18 employees b.) my voluntary work in an NGO helping children with disabilities c.) my involvement with the organization of student self-government." The trick is to package this information to appeal to the needs of the employer.

As the ability to package and re-package information is crucial to success in many jobs, the CV is a first practical test of your employability in such a role.[8] Part of this test is that you adapt your CV for every application, as your readers are curious whether you emphasize the points that are relevant for the specific job and organization you are applying to.

Microscopic attention to detail is another characteristic of your readers. They want to be sure that you can get everything right, when it matters. Managers want their employees to give them a finished and superior product, not something they need to check for potential mistakes. Their need for reliable employees is why any mistake in your CV may eliminate you from the list of candidates they will invite for an interview. Bad spelling means you did not check your application often enough. Inconsistent presentation of dates on your biography suggests you do not care

---

[8] Strictly speaking there is a distinction between the short résumé and the CV. The academic CV lists all detail and runs into several pages, up to 10. In practice, both serve the same purpose and the terms often are used interchangeably. The emphasis here is on the short version, because it is more likely to meet the needs of the reader.

about detail. Ugly formatting indicates that you cannot handle word-processing software. Any irregularity puts you at risk, as most employers value attention to detail.

Moreover, your readers most likely are <u>dismissive</u>. If they have an attractive position to offer, they may well have been overwhelmed by the number of applications. On one job I oversaw recruitment for, our organization received 300 applications. In another case, I oversaw an application process for 12 positions in Berlin, for which we received more than 600 qualified applications. If you gave each application five minutes, you would be working 50 hours, just for a first review.

To deal with the deluge of applications, many human resources managers use triage, a rapid division in three categories. One person will go through the stack and either:

1. shortlist stellar candidates after a scan of about 30 seconds;
2. immediately identify candidates for rejection, after about 45 seconds or less;
3. sort other application into a middle or borderline category that they will review later, or review as a broader team.

Separately, a second reviewer may check the rejections, to test for plausibility, but will again not spend more than a minute per application.

Depending on its length, the team works just with that shortlist for inviting candidates to the next stage, or keeps going back to review the borderline category in more detail, again putting candidates into shortlist or rejections, or further review by other team members. Given that your readers must be dismissive to handle the huge numbers, do not give them reasons to reject you through shortcomings such as glaring sloppiness.

Such attention to detail matters because of the <u>political and personal nature of hiring</u>, in many organizations. Many organizations of course prefer to hire on merit, but they also want to hire people they know they can rely on, and thus often go through personal recommendations, or hiring internally, or hiring people they previously got to know through internships. The personal nature of hiring matters in a number of ways to your application. If you apply from the outside, you give internal candidates an extra advantage if you weaken your application by making avoidable mistakes.

Sloppiness is political ammunition, as I once found when I was in a junior position and proposed rejecting a candidate because of formal mistakes in her application. My managers wanted to employ her because she brought degrees from renowned universities and references from well-connected senior officials. In the interview, the candidate had shown herself to be an unpleasant person to work with, with an aggressive streak. What to do? Problematic character traits are difficult to prove and if the interviewer points them out, it may look as if there was personal antipathy. As it happened, she had made major grammatical mistakes in her statement of purpose (in her native language). The formal mistakes made for a compelling case against the candidate: "if she can't get it right in her application, how can we trust her to get it right in other tricky situations?"

The political and personal angle can work to your advantage, if you are strategic. You can become that internal candidate, by doing good work that gets noticed, by working with and for an organization, potentially part-time, or by publishing articles. If, as a reader, you get an application from someone you had previously noticed for their good work, you will of course be positively inclined to give them a chance for an interview. Putting together your CV for an application can thus be an occasion to identify gaps, and think of ways (including voluntary engagement) on how to fill these gaps, over the coming months. When people know you, there is a better chance that they will look out for your application, and try to ensure that it makes it past the first review, in which dozens of applicants are eliminated, sometimes by junior personnel in the human resources department.

Lastly, readers will be <u>inquisitorial</u> once it comes to the interview. Here, following the second function of the CV, they will probe your arguments in more detail. They will, for example, ask you to expand on your arguments and subarguments, and check whether these are solid. Regarding your office management, they may ask how you have ensured that everyone in the team complied with the procedures you established. Follow-up questions allow your potential employers to establish whether your claim to competence is supported by relevant experience.

When talking about your work with children with disabilities, they may ask: "So where did you go to get outside support?" Here you should substantiate your argument that volunteering work is relevant to your application. The subargument could be that, among other things, the experience has developed your ability to mobilize partners. Regarding your education, they may check the subarguments on your argument that your education qualifies you for the job. "What was the most useful course you took at university?" With this question interviewers ask what *you* think your education was about – and how it demonstrates competence and commitment. Give an honest answer ("the course in History, because I had a great teacher who taught me how to write good essays – a skill I still find useful") that both makes sense for them and that fits your actual experience.

Given the inquisitorial nature of the interview, it should be clear (if it was not already) that your CV should make claims that you can substantiate. In a positive way, this is an opportunity to bring in items that previously you may not have thought about (such as voluntary engagement, or publishing on relevant issues). The inquisitorial nature of the interview suggests one good strategy for preparing for the interview: by annotating your own CV, with more information that demonstrates your competence, in relation to each of the biographical items. At the same time, given that you will be probed and questioned, stay away from claims you cannot back up in an interview. Inquisitorial readers most likely will spot incongruous claims on paper, given that they may easily have read more than one thousand CVs before they see yours, and they will certainly detect implausible claims in the interview.

- *Main Idea First: Within Each Item*

In this one instance, the principle of putting the main idea first does not apply directly. Yes, you should state your idea clearly. But you do not actually state your thesis in your CV, although you will do so in the cover letter that you send with the CV. It has, however, become somewhat of a practice in the United States to include an "objective". The objective is, so to speak, your thesis statement. I have seen some Georgians submit CVs in English with such an objective There are several problems with including an objective. The reader knows your objective and you have mentioned it in the cover letter, so you waste scarce space. Moreover, the objective increases risk. To write an objective well is not easy and does not get you much of an advantage, whereas doing it badly makes you look inept.

Still, the rule is that you state your information clearly, succinctly and as specific as possible.

- *Format*

The CV must contain who you are, how your activities have been relevant, where you have been in-between and how to get in touch with you. In practice, this means that you include name (don't put "CV" on top – everyone knows it is one); reliable contact details including, if possible, e-mail; education and work experience, skills, including languages and computer skills. You can include your profile on LinkedIn, especially if you have good recommendations.

In theory, you can put this information into any format and in any order that is written towards the purpose, for the reader, and that consequently states information clearly, succinctly and specifically. In practice, there are two formats that successfully meet these criteria: functional and reverse chronological.

In the **functional** format, you mention experience by category: Education, Professional Experience and Skills are always part of this. Skills – provided you have included them – can be divided by Computer Skills, Language Skills and potential other skills that are needed in your profession. Add other categories depending on your achievements and on the position to which you are applying: Awards, Publications, Certifications, and potentially Volunteer Experience, Interests or Hobbies. Mention the main things you have done, with emphasis on whatever is required for your job. If the job you are applying to requires the ability to work in a team, you can use your Interests to highlight relevant experience, for example, that you play in an orchestra. Similarly, if you have limited work experience, what you have done as a volunteer can be a good way of demonstrating your ability to make a difference. The EuroPass standard CV is a template for such a CV, and comes with solid instruction.[9]

Reverse chronological is a format in which you present your most recent experience first. You then list all the prior experiences. Reverse chronological is a good format because the most important information, your most recent job, is presented on top. If you add achievements as sub-points to your previous jobs, you can adapt them, highlighting the most relevant experience to the position you are applying for. In my case, for example, I do consulting, research, writing and training. I

---

[9] See http://europass.cedefop.europa.eu/about, retrieved November 20, 2015

emphasize relevant experience depending on the assignment I am submitting my CV for. In the lower third you have a section "Other Experiences" in which you can add whatever did not fit in well with the chronological order. If, for example, you have worked as a volunteer for ISFED (International Society for Fair Elections and Democracy) and observed elections with them over several years, you can list this here, as it is not part of the main narrative. Together with the sub-points, it will be this section which you adapt most as you tailor your CV for the specific application.

Although reverse chronological presents a clear narrative, its strict form is less suitable if many of your recent relevant activities overlapped – if, for example, you worked in different jobs while at university. For that reason, it is not suitable for the type of career that is fairly common in Georgia. Many students, for example, work at different positions while studying, over several years. In such cases, it is easier to organize information by category, i.e. into a functional CV. However, within each functional category, it is advisable to organize positions in reverse chronological order, e.g. list your most recent work experience first. (By now, most ministerial biographies on websites, for example, are presented in reverse chronological format.)

A third type that still has some circulation is the **chronological** format. It starts from the beginning, i.e. from your school education and then traces your subsequent development. The chronological format puts the most important information last and gives the least relevant information first. In my view, it violates our main principles and I would avoid this format, unless you are specifically asked to present your CV in this way. It is, however, useful for very short biographies, for example in a conference program, or to describe an artist's development.

Whichever format you choose (to learn how they work, you can try both), your readers will be enthusiastic if you can keep to one page. Brevity is the first test of your competence: how to pack the relevant information onto one page. Your readers do not need too much detail. They primarily want to check whether you have the right qualifications and are not over- or underqualified.

Exceptionally, longer CVs are acceptable, if your audience needs more detail to assess your capacity, for example because you need to explain achievements in more detail, or when the context will not be familiar to your readers. Yet this remains the exception, more suitable at a mid-career point when connecting to people outside the established context. The more succinct you are, the better, and your most recent position anyway is the most relevant item, whereas earlier experience is less relevant.

Regarding your achievements, the less the reader knows, the more you should tell him. If you have been in organizations which everybody knows, holding a position that everyone is familiar with, you need little additional description. Everyone easily grasps university study. But if you have done marketing for a small start-up company in the Netherlands, you should describe the activities. The usual rule remains that you emphasize specific results. Describe them in active voice, with short, terse and meaningful statements. Quantify achievements wherever possible.

For example, an applicant for the position of an assistant marketing manager for a small wine exporter may write:

May '15	*Telavi Natural Wines LTD*
- June '16	Assistant Marketing Manager

- managed and maintained ongoing marketing campaigns in Europe
- identified new sales opportunities for our wines and personally placed flagship product in four new outlets in the US, and two in Japan
- increased sales by $27 000, increasing company sales by 9%, in addition to general growth

This is a powerful statement. The candidate has focused on information that appears relevant, and gives an idea of her ability for the desired position Although the sum is not a lot of money measured against the total market, it appears to be significant in the context of this small (fictional) company, and shows that this candidate has may develop further. It certainly is preferable to

- "responsible for new sales"

The $ 27 000 mentioned above are better than a potential $ 100 000 hidden behind the bland phrase of "responsible for..." (which is anyway a passive, and not active, statement). Generalities only work if they relate to a job that the candidate held several years ago, and if the more recent descriptions are more detailed. Always offer a clear image to the reader, something that is easy to visualize.

When writing your descriptions, put yourself into the position of an inquisitive reader: you want the text to be specific, short and clear, with an emphasis on activity, numbers and results. You want to see that the person writing the application can be precise and to the point. After looking through dozens of applications, you are tired of standard phrases and will prefer quantified substance to abstract generalities. Moreover, you will want to know how previous experience may relate to the requirements of the position.

As you put together your CV, bear all this in mind. To be convincing, you should keep the descriptions in as neutral a tone as possible and avoid turning them into a personal story. As a rule, omit the first person singular ("I managed...") and use, wherever possible, third person.

Don't say "I have great/outstanding/excellent skills of...", as you take risks with such a claim. If your skills are outstanding, you will have achievements to prove it and these will speak for themselves. "Show, don't tell..." is a good principle to remind you to emphasize results.

Under Education, mention your degrees, of course. Put grades if you are convinced that they distinguish your performance and are an indication that you did work hard. Otherwise, just mention the completion of the degree, possibly listing the areas of specialisation. If you have not yet completed your course, include your expected date of graduation. Put in anything else that you think the reader should know about you, e.g. relevant coursework that would not be assumed as part of your specialization.

Mention your interests if they relate to the job or if you have little experience so far. Only mention interests that indicate skills and distinguish you from others. Reading, travel, music are not suitable, because they are commonplace and may describe passive consumption. Your cat, too, can travel and listen to Mozart. An interest in "18th-century Irish poetry", however, may be worth mentioning, if you have something engaging to say about it. Your inquisitorial interviewers may well take you up on it – to make you feel at ease and because they want to see how you talk about things you love. If you sparkle on such issues, they may well take an even stronger interest in you joining their team. Again, make sure you only mention items that are relevant. I once interviewed someone who had listed reading and literature as an interest, but struggled to identify her favourite book – nothing came to mind.

Make sensible use of the space on the page. Balancing white space and writing is important for readability. The further back you go, the less information is needed. If, for example, you should mention recent activities by the month, you can restrict yourself to years if items – such as School Education – go back several years.

If you have people who can write you a professional reference (always try to get one for your work), and references were not specifically requested, you can mention that "References available upon request". It is, however, not obligatory to mention this, since it is assumed that you can provide references. If, for some special reason, you write a longer CV, you can supply the names of the referees, their full addresses including e-mail and the type of relationship you had, for example whether they were your teachers, employers, or, in some circumstances, your professional colleagues and so on. You should make sure, of course, that these people are prepared to give you a reference and that they will have good things to say about you.

- *Procedure*

Define the job you are applying for and consider what responsibilities it involves. Decide whether you want the job and in what specific ways you are qualified for it. Do research the job thoroughly, identifying the skills that are needed. Determine both the general requirements of the job and its day-to-day tasks and responsibilities. If you have an actual job notice, study it carefully. Highlight the key terms/phrases used so that you can tailor your CV and cover letter to suit the employer's requirements. Think about your potential employers' needs, attitudes and goals.

Research the organization in general. If you know people who work at the organization, or worked there previously, ask them about their experience, and about the position, after you have done preparatory research. If you can determine the organization's philosophy or specialization, you will be able to explain in more detail how you are qualified and why you are interested in working for them. Characterize the organization (in the context of this position) with 3-5 adjectives. The better you understand what an employer wants, the better you will be able to write a CV that gets you invited to the interview. Your task here, however, is not just to repeat all the available information to yourself – it is about analysing, characterising and summarizing so that you can define how specifically you will try to convince your reader.

Assemble your own experiences that match up with the requirements – or that show that you have the potential: jobs, internships, voluntary work, projects, extracurricular activities, education. Write them down on a sheet.

Group the information sensibly: analyse and synthesize it. Identify the transferable skills that you have gained from your experience, and see how it is relevant to the job you are applying to. Find detailed descriptions that demonstrate your achievements, emphasizing the results. Deviating from normal practice, you can already begin to type details into the computer now, as the CV itself is a kind of outline to start with.

Order this information. Make your final choice on what is relevant. Choose the functional or the reverse chronological format, and make sure that it is consistent.

Review thoroughly. Does it look clean? Is it well structured? Is every item an argument? Print it out, as seeing it on paper often gives you a fresh perspective. Read the CV aloud, and potentially read it backwards, forcing yourself to read each word to check for mistakes. Show it to someone who has experience. Re-check it, if possible, after a day or two.

If invited for an interview, take two copies of your CV. One to offer the interviewer and one for yourself. Most likely they have a copy, but if you bring one it illustrates that you are prepared. On your copy, prepare for the interview by writing after every item in what way this has developed you, what you have learnt from the experience.

Keep all your CVs saved so that you can quickly adapt them. It makes sense to keep one long "Master-CV", running up to several pages, listing everything in some detail and adapting this to a one-page CV for specific applications. Once you have a good master version, it does not take long to adapt future CVs for applications (though you should always adapt them).

- ### *Remember: Details, Principles, Long-Term Planning*

Having a perfect CV does not get you a job, but a bad one guarantees that you will not get it. To eliminate mistakes, show your CV to several people. You may get divergent (and irritating) comments, but if one out of every four comments is useful and catches a mistake, the outside review has been well worth it.

Keep to the principles. Consider the audience. The second principle helps you when you encounter additional questions. Should you include your date of birth? It depends on the audience. Many continental Europeans are used to seeing a date of birth on the CV, and it is part of the EuroPass format. In the United States, dates of birth are considered inappropriate, as candidates should not be disadvantaged because of age. Whether that custom makes much sense is another question, as the approximate age can be estimated from degrees or work experience. But the custom it is, and you demonstrate awareness by complying.

Should you include a photograph? Again, second principle, consider the audience. In the United States, a photograph should not be included, as there is the view that people should be hired on their merits, not on looks. There are additional concerns that photographs can disadvantage minority candidates. In continental Europe, photos often are included. If you include a photo, make it professionally appropriate and friendly. I have seen anything from photos that look as if they were taken just after an arrest, across men in their sleeveless muscle shirts, to sultry poses that were appropriate for dating sites. Remember that your LinkedIn photo matters, too, and check your privacy settings on social media before you apply, or make sure the content is presentable.

Present your information clearly, cleanly, conservatively, succinctly and be specific. Quantify your actual achievements wherever that is possible. Make sure you are remarkable because you demonstrate your competence and commitment.

Keep the formatting of your CV simple and use a standard program. When sending your CV by e-mail, try to use a PDF so that retains its original format. (Most modern word processing programs allow you to turn a document into PDF, through an export function.)

Be perfect. Follow the job announcements to the letter and under all circumstances send in your application before the deadline. Here is what someone wrote, who was suggesting that I should emphasize this point as much as possible: "giving our example, we once asked people to send in one-page CVs and by e-mail only, nevertheless we kept getting two- and three-page CVs by fax, some would just bring it in, etc. I can live with that, but some employers (like my boss) find it irritating and immediately eliminate 'disobedient' applicants."

Try applying for jobs that are hard to get, but remain realistic. Your actual experience is your best guide for what positions you are likely to be considered for. Keep going, even if you have suffered a few disappointments. Success, as Winston Churchill pointed out, consists of going from failure to failure without loss of enthusiasm.

Think of your CV a long time before you apply: do things that you genuinely enjoy and become good at, including voluntary work. There are many good initiatives in Georgia who can use competent people to help them. Many media outlets will take a well-researched and well-written piece on an issue you are interested in. This creates an opportunity for you to get closer to the kinds of jobs and people you are interested in. Use your time and accumulate experiences that you can put on your CV, even if they require you to do detail-oriented and repetitive tasks. ("Anything that is truly interesting is 90% boring", is how the writer Elizabeth Gilbert once put it.) Such work demonstrates commitment and is a long-term investment.

Read this section thoroughly. Having been involved in hiring people for 17+ years, I think that most of what you need is included, with some additional material on cover letters in the next section. When you have a question, go back to the first and second principles. Based on these, take your decisions on your CV. Employers want you to excel at taking good decisions, and with your CV you can demonstrate your skill.

Business Letter

How to introduce yourself or an idea to someone.

- ***Purpose: Get Outside Contacts to Act – Principle I***

In a business letter, you specifically address one person (or a group of persons) to get them to do something. Invest your time to exactly define this purpose. Visualize what you want the target audience to do. Consider whether that visualization is realistic and how it can be made even more realistic, for example by identifying common interests.

Letters may of course have radically different purposes. In making an offer, you want the reader to recognise the attractiveness of your product. When complaining to an organization, you want the reader to change or even to offer redress. When asking someone to pay their bill, you want them to follow up quickly. In a conflict, you may want the other side to agree to settle, as you make them understand that your legal position is strong. You decide what you want to achieve and then to choose the style of writing that is most likely to succeed – rather than writing to express what you feel.

- ***Busy and Impatient Readers – Principle II***

Keep it short and simple. Most of your readers will be busy, impatient, maybe even egotistical in that they want to immediately see what is in it for them. Readers will like your letters and like working with you if you can present your information clearly. Try to put yourself in the position of the reader. It helps you to understand how you are supposed to write.

Writing from the reader's perspective is especially helpful when the situation is emotionally charged, for example when you demand redress after something went wrong. Such difficult letters should be written so that the reader is encouraged to react constructively and not to become angry or hostile because you pushed him into a corner.

Again, characterize your likely readers with 3-5 adjectives. If the person you are writing to is upset, for example, you may want to adjust your tone accordingly.

- ### *Give your Main Idea First: Action*

In professional letters, you indeed state the main idea first. Tell the readers in the beginning why you are writing to them. You do this close to the top of the page, where there is a line in which you summarise what the letter is about. You should repeat the main idea in the first sentence of the letter, though you can use the introduction formula to set up what you need to say. Make sure that any person who will look at the letter, including an assistant, will immediately understand what the letter is about. They can then pass the letter to the person who is responsible, to ensure you get a response.

- ### *Indicate Specific Action at the End*

At the end of the letter, say what the next specific step will be. This can be something like: "I am looking forward to hearing from you." Yet it is even better if you can indicate the specific action you request (giving formal agreement; nominating representatives to a task force; removing an obstacle to implementation). If you require action within a certain time frame, make sure this date is displayed prominently.

If you want to maintain control of the dynamic, you can say "Unless you object, we will call you to discuss this issue with you in the next few days." Or just: "I will call you to find out your views on this issue in a few days." The exact tone depends on your relationship with the reader.

Leave enough time to reply to you before you call: three working days (plus time for delivery of the letter, if go the classical route). If the person does not want to hear from you, he can say so in writing. When calling them, you will often try to get an appointment to discuss the issue in person. Try to make sure that at each point it is easier for them to say "yes" than to say "no".

Be specific about the expected action in the last line if you need to nudge people to do something – pay a bill, follow up on a contract, provide you with information, or whatever else it is. This helps them to move to action. Do not end on a note of threat ("Pay, or we will complain to all business associations."). You want your counterpart to be in let's-get-this-solved-mode rather than to turn stubborn, as people often do under threat, against their interests. End on a co-operative note and ask them to deliver. If you are considering taking more serious action explain this in neutral terms. You can say in the body of the text that you always require your partners to fulfil the contracts and cannot afford to make exceptions.: "Therefore we would be very grateful to you if you could deliver the materials as originally agreed by the end of the month."

If matters escalate, always consider delegating the conflict to someone else, either in your organization or a lawyer. Conflicts consume more energy than most people expect when they get into one. You want to send people forward who specialize in solving them. Hopefully conflicts will remain rare, and to keep them the exception you should work to de-escalate whenever possible.

- *Typical Format*

The main thing about the format is that it should make sense: it should organize the necessary information clearly. The advice here is for old-school letters, rather than for e-mail. Yet such formal letters today still often are written, and delivered via courier (giving them extra weight, nowadays) or attached to e-mail. Adapt to context as appropriate. Here, at any rate, is what formal letters look like:

1.) Your name and address
This format has developed because many letterheads are pre-printed and hence are at the top of the page.

2.) The address of the person you are writing to - two lines below
If you are writing to a company, try to identify who is responsible. If you address it to someone, she becomes responsible to properly direct it and you can call that person to follow up on where the letter is. Put the organization first, the person second. This sequence indicates that the letter is primarily addressed to the official position. Letters that appear to be private correspondence (from the envelope) may be left unopened if the person you are writing to is away on a business trip or vacation. Check, however, standard practice in your field: for ease of addressing, people often use person, firm, location, and this can also be appropriate when addressing the head of an organization.[10]

3.) The date – on the same line as the address, on the right side
You put it here because it is a good use of empty space. At the same time, you have the date high up on the letter, which helps in sorting and filing it.

4.) Regarding - two lines further down
This should say in a few succinct words what the letter refers to, possibly with the relevant file-number, and be as specific as possible.

---

[10] To write e-mail to a person whose address you cannot find, check the naming conventions in an organization (for me likely versions would be: hgutbrod; gutbrodh; gutbrod; hans – once an organization has a rule, they often apply it consistently) One nifty way of writing, if you are not sure, is that you enter the most likely name in the address line, and then put likely alternate wordings into BCC – the person will then likely receive the e-mail, but not immediately see that you tried alternative spellings.

5.) Personally address the person you are writing to – two lines further down
Always good to have a name, otherwise go for the still-awkward "Dear Sir or Madam" or "Dear Sales Manager". ("To Whom It May Concern" is too general for use in a letter.)

6.) Body text – one-and-a-half lines below
The first paragraph is on why you are writing. The following paragraphs explain this, roughly in essay form, or in situation-complication-resolution, if the letter is brief. The last short paragraph is on the specific action to be taken, including all necessary elements of the action formula.

7.) Greetings – set off slightly from the main text, a bit to the right.
Find the appropriate form – if you are writing to someone who is more senior, be rigorously formal, without becoming artificially stiff. If you write to someone who is junior, you can be informal. "Best regards" remains perhaps the most versatile salutation.

8.) Signature by hand
Ideally have a hand-written signature, even for letters that are attached to e-mail. You can, for example, scan your signature and then paste it into documents.

- **Procedure**

Unless the text is simple, go through the standard procedure of writing things: DAGOR. Using the procedure is quicker, because you think before you write, rather than rewriting. (Paper-and-pencil DAGOR can often be done in 3-5 minutes, and establish a good structure for your document.) Keep the text short. One-and-half pages is the maximum length for a typical letter. If it is longer, reorganize the material into a separate document and use your letter to introduce this longer document, and to draw the reader's attention to the main features.

There are some exceptions to the two-page maximum. Lawyers use longer letters in legal disputes. The length is needed to set out a case, provide evidence and to formally rebut claims made by the other side. The purpose of such letters often is to provide a legal record of the disagreement, rather than to engage or convince the person you are writing to. In other words: the overwhelming number of letters you write should stay short.

Experienced writers usually ask someone to check their letters before sending, as their experience has taught them that it is easy to overlook a mistake. Show to your readers that you care about the quality of your relationship by sending high-quality documents.

- ***Cover Letters***

Cover letters are the letters you send with your application. The cover letter complements your CV. (Read the section on CVs, too.) Cover letters set out a summary of why you should be hired. The cover letter states this thesis – which is substantiated by the arguments on the CV. The character of the thesis and the relationship of the thesis to the arguments is the same as in an essay. The thesis is a succinct summary of the arguments. Together, they form one unit.

The format of cover letters is similar to business letters in most respects. If you can write good cover letters, you will find it easy to draft a compelling business letter. Cover letters should answer three questions:

1.) What are you applying for (and where did you hear about it)?
2.) Why specifically are you qualified for the job?
3.) Why are you interested in it?

The first question should be answered in the first sentence. You do a favour to personnel managers when you tell them how you heard about this job opening, because they want to know where they need to advertise.

You can be more flexible when answering the next two questions – but you must be specific. Use DAGOR. What do they require? What specifically do you offer? Assemble what is *specifically* relevant: detailed knowledge of regulatory environment, three years' experience in income tax disputes, ability to work to tight deadlines, strength in finding original marketing solutions, ability to work under pressure – or just high reliability and being a good team player. In response to the question about your qualification, develop a thesis as you do with an essay.

Your thesis should be tightly focused, specific and convincing. The thesis should connect your past achievements to the requirements of the position you are applying to. Do not just say that you were "great" in your last job; instead, say, for example, that you organized the logistics for three successful conferences with more than 30 international guests each. By citing specific achievements, you demonstrate that you can focus and this will work in your favour. To be convincing, the thesis should also remain realistic. Experienced interviewers easily identify exaggerated claims in an interview, and likely may spot them in the cover letter already.

Present yourself as a solution, not just as a bundle of skills. Remember the saying that people want holes in the ground, not shovels. In other words, they want a result (the hole), not an instrument. Below is an example of a shovel, a typical sentence from an unsophisticated cover letter:

> "I am a fully trained lawyer with some international background working for a Berlin-based consultancy active in the field of energy regulation. As a regulatory consultant, I have advised the management…"

The next version presents a hole in the ground. There are no sparks of brilliance, but it is a powerful pitch, especially if the subsequent sentences support this claim:

> "As a fully qualified lawyer I bring the detailed knowledge of regulatory frameworks and administrative structures that this position will require. In my capacity as a regulatory consultant…"

Make sure the paragraphs themselves are tightly integrated units, with no redundant information.

When describing your interest in the job -- the third question you are answering in the cover letter -- you keep to roughly similar requirements. Be specific and genuine. Employers want people who are enthusiastic about their job. People are committed to learn and improve when they are enthusiastic – and such people are fun to work with. If you show potential employers that you will enjoy the job, they are much more likely to hire you. Identify why specifically you are interested in the job. Again, if you cannot think of any genuine reason (outside earning a salary) you either have a bad day, or shouldn't apply to that position. Ask someone with good judgement for advice: show them the job description and ask them what they think your strengths are in applying for the position. This paragraph, too, should be short and concise.

You can mention major weaknesses that you yourself have identified – if you compensate them with strengths. Be sure to give a strength that is more powerful than your weakness. If, for example, the description says that they want someone with three years' job experience you can say: "Although I only have worked two years, I already have experience in managing staff and have helped to administer a budget of $35,000." Such a statement works in your favour, because it shows that you are aware of your limitations and of how you can compensate for them.

Qualification and genuine interest will then constitute what your CV sets out to prove. As mentioned above, your cover letter highlights the strengths that you will substantiate in your CV.

In the cover letter, you should be able to describe your suitability in two or three paragraphs. The more you talk, the less plausible the connection between you and the position will seem to the reader. Remember that the cover letter is a summary. After reading your cover letter, the reader should have formed a distinct one- or two-sentence explanation why you are an attractive candidate.

As in an essay, you do not take the reader through a story. Do not list your background, high-school education, university education and so on. Your application will likely be discarded if you make this basic mistake.

Cover letters must be a bit like Mount Kazbegi: impressive, nice to look at, and with lots of white space. With both the mountain and a good letter one immediately gets the main idea. Cover letters must be flawless. Your readers don't want to employ someone who makes careless mistakes.

A good way to end a cover letter is to say "I look forward to hearing from you." If you are applying to a professional organization, they will contact you (unless otherwise noted on the job description). I used to recommend that you can follow up with a call after two weeks, but have never heard of this yielding a result for anyone I know. You are, realistically, at the mercy of the human resources processes, and if you invest effort anywhere, do it over the years, to get to know people in many organizations, who will be interested in you joining their team.

- ***Remember: Collect Good Samples, Collaborate***

Letters are a direct form of address. They deserve great attention and it takes experience to write them well. If you come across letters that you think are excellent, keep them, collect them in a folder and regularly look at them. What makes them great?

Identify someone in your office who is better at writing letters than you are and find out what they are doing right. How do they manage to phrase tricky issues in diplomatic language?

Co-operate. Communication is not a hermit's enterprise. Ask each other for help and show your letters to others before you send them. You yourself may have become blind to the shortcomings of your letter, as your brain refers to its own memory, rather than the document itself. You need someone who reads it for the first time. If absolutely no one is available, read the text out loud – hearing you will get another impression of the sentences. Let some time pass and read it again.

The ability to write good letters brings success. If you can write good letters, your advice will be sought, you will draft important documents, and you can help your organization have an impact.

Press Release

How to inform the public about your activities.

- **Purpose: Engage the Public, or Parts of Public – Principle I**

The purpose of your press release is to draw public attention to what you are doing – to your organization, its activities, or its views. You use the press release to promote classical media coverage of your work, as well as promoting your work directly through your website and social media presence. As with previous documents, you define what the purpose of your press release will be. Visualize the intended result.

As a citizen initiative, you may want to show the public that you have achieved a that air quality data now is publicly accessible, around the clock. The intended result may be that you want more people to join your next initiative to push for cleaner fuel standards, and to sign up for your subscription list, ideally right after they read about your success.

As a research institute, you may want to highlight your recent study that shows five proven (and inexpensive) strategies to raise educational achievement in secondary schools. You will want policy-makers, researchers and journalists to join the launch event, and to be excited about your findings and to talk about them, to themselves and others, to discuss how they can implement these ideas.

As a university or training college, you may want to show that your graduating class has achieved encouraging success. Your aim here may be to make current students feel good about themselves, and to attract more good students and qualified staff in the future, and for some of them to join your graduating event, or at least to sign up for your monthly newsletter.

A government ministry can highlight its progress in introducing a policy that improves the lives of citizens. As one of the simplest measures of success, you may want more "likes" on Facebook. Yet beyond that, you want citizens to talk about how this ministry is doing good work, and to be more supportive of that ministry, perhaps to be reflected in future surveys as well. Ideally you want that good conversation to reach other ministries and be noticed at the very top of government. Such a result makes your minister more popular, and your department more popular with the minister, making it easier to get resources from her in the future.

Actual motivations will have additional dimensions to those mentioned here, for example you often want to reach several audiences at the same time. Yet the overall idea is the same. You want an action, as the result: people to come to sign up, to come to an event, to talk positively, or (if you are a company) to sign up to a service or buy a product you are offering. Any public-facing organization therefore has some reason to communicate with the public – and a press release is a good tool for doing so.[11]

- *Diverse, Indifferent, Distracted Readers – Principle II*

As your key potential readers are media professionals, you should make the press release attractive for journalists. Providing good material for media professionals includes the usual requirements, such as writing concise and specific prose that avoids complicated language. Meet the journalists' specific needs. Be easy to contact (including in late evenings) and keep to the deadlines they give you, as they must produce and publish in their own schedule.

---

[11] Because many media outlets are underresourced, there also is the category of the article that is purchased. Here we show how you can try to help journalists write without having to pay them.

A well written press release makes the job of a journalist easier by providing key information and quotations that are properly sourced and verified. This information is organized in a manner that makes it easy to understand and adapt for publication by the news media. Even if a reporter is unable to attend your event or read your publication, they have enough information to at least publish a brief report on what you are announcing.[12]

More broadly, three adjectives come to mind when characterizing the readers of press releases: diverse, indifferent, distracted.

The readers of press releases typically are diverse. In addition to your target group, there may be several additional groups reading your press release. Your press release (a) should work for the target group, or groups (which in your specific case you will characterize with 3 to 5 adjectives), (b) ideally appeals to non-target groups, and (c) shouldn't annoy anyone else. For that reason, too, it's good to keep press releases short. With a short press release, there is less content for anyone to object to, and less text that needs to be reviewed and edited. Sure, some people or groups will object to anything you do ("haters gonna hate", as the saying goes), but avoid attracting extra attention or passing out ammunition. Keeping your press release focused, on one issue, with well-established language, helps to reach the right audience, and avoid distraction.

Your readers will be indifferent, too. Even your target group may well be indifferent. Their indifference likely will be one of your key challenges. There are other things happening. Why should they pay any attention to you? Your press release needs to be relevant to their direct concerns. The writing needs to be

---

[12] In our own work, Transparify's press release and first page of a report became the basis of quotes that the Financial Times used for a report on our work, without interviewing us. See: http://bit.ly/Transparify-PR-2015 and http://bit.ly/FT-Article.

excellent. Beyond the writing, too, personal connections can help, to ensure that people look at your press release (maybe after you called them, or told them at an event a few days earlier that you would get in touch). Having an established reputation, and establishing your absolute credibility in the field further increase your chances. Yet even then, the press release needs to make a difference for them, to transcend their indifference.

Your readers likely will be distracted, too. Your aim is to get your readers (or at least as many of them as possible) to act, not just to notice. For this, your press release needs to make them care. Ideally, there should be an emotional connection that moves them towards the intended action. The emotional angle can often be low-key, and rely on curiosity or sympathy or human connection. One of the reasons why press releases usually quote people is because it is easier to connect to people rather than to abstract issues. That connection should be genuine, and sustainable. Many people resent and shut out dramatic appeals.

So, more than ever, characterize your specific target audience with three to five adjectives. Develop an approach or angle that will appeal to them. The test, as you may have heard before, is in the "so what?" question. Why should your audience notice, and why should they care? Identify angles that matter to your readers. Finding this angle takes time. Look at the box below, with fictional examples, to see how topics turn into angles.

Ministry Of Health offers new registration precedure for pregnant benefits	Pregnant women can now register online, for quicker access to benefits
Ministry of Internal Affairs now with new emergency rescue capacity	Faster and better rescue in Georgian mountains, with ne MIA helicopter
New cardio medic emergency ambulance in service	New ambulance can save up to 45 lives per year
Educational Research Institute presents annual report & results of research into student exam scores	Ambrolauri school again top in tests, according to ERI report
Survey shows what Tblissi residents think	Tbilissi residents want better air quality and smoother traffic, according to new survey
Construction industry association adopts binding standard	Neighbors to benefit from quieter & cleaner construction, says industry body

To appeal to our readers, we emphasize results, focus on what is attractive, and try to phrase positively. This emphasis may bring at least some of them out of their indifference.

The better angle emphasizes the practical difference that you made, or are about to make. These results will make people take note. Often the focus are the beneficiaries, rather than the acting institutions. Most readers will be more interested in what the results are, rather than in who is active.

Moreover, we focus on what is attractive, and try to create a compelling image. Thus, the focus may be selective. The "new emergency rescue capacity" may have various aspects, including cave rescue, but the helicopter likely is the most visually appealing, and thus worth emphasizing. In focusing on the attraction, we often omit detail, such as leaving out the cardio-medic specification from the headline, to draw readers to the news about saved lives. Relevant detail follows later.

To draw in readers, we typically use positive phrasing. The construction industry, in this fictional example, highlights "quieter and cleaner construction", rather than saying "less noise and less pollution", as noise and pollution still are negatively associated. When the British construction industry set up a body, they called it the "Considerate Constructors Scheme", not the "Less Awful Building Sites". I am exaggerating for effect, to illustrate that little tweaks can help your institution to present itself, even if you are in the tough position that people want your results (as in apartments, or road safety) but not your process (building sites, or enforcement and fines). Broadly in the same style, the survey results headline with what people want – cleaner air and smoother traffic – rather than how respondents characterized air as horrible and rush-hour traffic as a disaster.

The examples above illustrate how you can find an angle, in a simplified context. You may well have alternative and better suggestions, and depending on the audience your tone and emphasis will vary. For your own press release, you will arrive at the best version by analyzing your audience. Ideally get to know the audience long before you draft this one press release, and listen to them (rather than talking).

Once you have the angle, build the entire press release around it. The content of your press release must cohere with the angle you take. In practice a good angle is not an obstacle to writing – as is true for a good thesis in an essay, an angle focuses what you are going to say and gives you a direction that makes it easier to write. You can easily expand on the angle, for example including additional information on the new emergency rescue team of the MIA, or giving much more detail on your research on the test performance of schools, or explaining additional findings from your survey of Tbilisi residents.

If you meet the needs of media professionals, they will work with you again. Journalists and specifically editors are grateful for information because they have the difficult task of filling empty outlet slots – pages or minutes – each day. As is true for many other fields: think of your press work as a relationship, not a transaction.

- *Main Idea First: Title, First Paragraph*

In a press release you twice put the main idea first. First, you capture the main idea in the title. The title catches the attention by conveying the essence of what you have to say and should get the reader (and journalist or editor) to be interested in what you are saying. Again, this takes time and hard work, and may well be a compromise, or selective, as you can't cover all aspects. What makes it easier is having clearly defined what you want to achieve.

The first paragraph in the press release should answer to the action formula: who does what how when where why. The reader should get an answer to these questions after reading the first paragraph. You put the most important element first. If the emphasis is on a person or organization, "who" comes first. If you are writing about an event or problem, "what" is first.

Who: David Lordkipanidze receives prestigious archaeological prize …

What: Famous Kakabadze painting re-discovered …

In the press release, there is no formal introduction of situation, complication, resolution because that would prevent you from going directly to the issue.

There is another reason why the main idea needs to come first. Press releases may have to be cut to fit into a publication. They are cut from the back. Make sure that no important information (except for the background) is at the back of the press release. Instead you just expand on what you said in the first paragraph. The last part of the press release should only contain secondary information, what we described as subarguments or supports, in structural terms.

Editors say that press releases should be written like a pyramid, as in the pyramid we described in the section on structure: the idea is that you can cut from below and the pyramid still retains its shape, with the most important information is right at the top.

- *Potential Occasions*

Some typical occasions in which you could publish a press release could include the following:

- Press Conferences – should always be accompanied by a press release
- Good news – of any sort
- Milestones – "a thousand eye-patients treated with innovative laser surgery"

- Records – "biggest harvest / export / production / exhibition / local festival"
- Firsts – "new solar water-heaters in Tsalka region to supply more than 800 households"; "new hybrid busses to serve on traditional #17 bus line"; "first export of Georgian feijoa to Germany"
- Charity Events – concert, fair, market
- Community service – any news, including by company or state institution undertaking a community-service event
- Events open to the public – readings, concerts, plays, exhibitions
- Release of a book or report – coupled with a launch event "[Publishing house] launches new handbook for professional communication"
- Offering internships, apprenticeships or training programs – "National Bank offers internships to economics students"
- Offering a new product or service – "Barbar starts new Georgian recycling plant"

Not all of the descriptions above are yet specific for the reader, so the angle may still need to be refined. These are just some of the possible occasions for which you can use a press release. Obviously, some of these occasions may be combined. Also, you can create the event that justifies the press release – a company may, for example, help create the biggest khatchapuri to have a highlight for an event. Do work to add sufficient substance for people to care.

- *Typical Format*

A successful press release allows a reporter to quickly understand what you are publicizing, why it is 'newsworthy', and extract key facts without having to engage in time-consuming research themselves. If they are interested in the subject your press release allows them to move quickly beyond the most basic questions, saving valuable time. All the key information should thus be upfront, and very accessible.

One key feature of press releases is that they typically quote one or several people. Quotations make the text better to read, as the reader can picture a person saying something, and may connect to the person on some level, too. Mention the full name, title and, if applicable, the organization of the person being quoted. The person quoted usually is the public face of the organization or of that program or project, i.e. some kind of director. Additionally or alternatively, you can quote a person you helped, or a client, or supporter, or worker who is affected by (ideally: benefits from) your news. Do make sure that the quotation is accurate and that the person you quote has signed off on them being quoted. (It can be tempting to take a good quote, for example, from an internal report in which someone expressed gratitude, though the person has not consented to being cited.) Your organization gets bad publicity if the customer expressing enthusiasm in the press release later complains that she has been misquoted.

In today's social media context, try to add one or several attractive visuals. These can be photographs, or a data visualization that is striking and engaging. Visuals are good for sharing on social media, so select them accordingly. Good photos display activity that can easily be recognized, and data, if visualized, should be easy to understand. Photos get lost or mixed up, so save any attached photo with a name that says as much as possible. And again, ask the persons shown on the photo (and the photographer) whether they agree with you using it. If you have photographer friends on social media, you will see regularly see complaints about finding their photographs being used, without receiving any compensation (or acknowledgement). Ideally, you collect good visuals of your organization, to which you have the full rights, in a shared folder, so that you have material you can use quickly, when you want to publish a press release.

- Organization, possibly your standard letterhead or logo.
- Title: powerful, few words, communicating the angle

- Dateline: Date and location from which you are sending this (Tbilisi, Kutaisi).
- Body text in clear paragraphs; paragraphs spaced apart at least 1.5 lines.
- One page, if other material needs to be added, link to it separately; in exceptional cases, two pages (if there are two pages, write 1 of 2 and 2 of 2 underneath).
- If you want readers to take specific action, you may repeat what they need to do at the very end: the exact time and location of where you launch the report; how to register for a media event; how to access the website for registration.
- Write "End" in the middle of the page where text ends.
- Give the name for the press contact and as much contact information as possible with phone numbers where you can be reached directly throughout the relevant period, including evenings as journalists work late into the night. Include your time-zone, if you are sending internationally. Be available and always have relevant information with you, so that you can give the journalist more information. If you have interesting things to say, journalists may turn your short release into an even bigger story. Give e-mail and, if you have one, your organization's web page, and potentially your Skype address if it is an international story. Update your web page, so that relevant information can be found.
- At the end give a small background statement that describes your organization or project to journalists. Sometimes this can be just two lines about your organization. Set this background description apart visually by using a different font or format.

- *Procedure*

Follow the same DAGOR procedure as in writing an essay. Put particular stress on defining your purpose and on your target audience, as well as on the media outlets that you want to reach out to.

To prepare your press release, in addition to DAGOR, typical questions you could ask yourself include:

- What do we want to achieve?
- Which target groups do we need to reach to achieve this? How to characterize them with 3-5 adjectives?
- What outlets allow us to reach the target audience? When, where and how do they publish or broadcast?
- Who makes the relevant decision? Editor? Journalist, supplementary editor, special reporters?
- Do we have some direct contact to them?
- Do we know free-lance journalists?

Time your releases well. Some events should be published several times to attract attention. A few days before the event you could send a brief press release emphasizing the most exciting aspect of what will happen, and then another press release on the day of. Watch for your timing, so that you don't get overshadowed by other events. In 2016, I was involved in launching a report focused on the United Kingdom – two days after Brexit happened. Like most, we had assumed that Brexit would not happen. Our report still got attention, but much less than it otherwise might have achieved. We ideally should have launched several weeks earlier, but got that wrong. You can't control all crises, but make sure you don't coincide with timing in a bad way

As you would review the plan for an essay, ask yourself at the end of planning for your press release "How are readers going to relate to this and will they be able to connect?" If you are not sure, find out why and, if necessary, amend as necessary.

Do a last check on who else you should include or notify, such as partners or contributors. Forgetting a partner can cause trouble. We once did a study on social capital for a major development donor, and the online edition of the Economist picked it up. On the morning of publication, at 10 a.m. there was much enthusiasm from the donor. By 11:30, they realized that they had not been named as the sponsor of the research, and I received an angry e-mail, demanding that I should push the Economist to include the sponsor (and ideally a disclaimer that they did not necessarily endorse all the content). I could not deliver on that demand, as of course I did not have editorial control. The success of being mentioned turned into recrimination from the donor, and the project ended on a bitter note.

Whatever the donor attitudes, the final mistake was mine. After hearing from the Economist, I should have informed the donor, offering that they could be cited (without a cumbersome disclaimer), or decline to be in the story. The story illustrates how important it is to think of your partners before publication – and that even with years of communications experience, you still have opportunities to learn from your mistakes.

The story may illustrate, too, that phone calls in advance are a useful part of getting a press release on track. Successful press releases are about writing and talking – as it is through direct contact that you can launch successfully.

- *Remember: Help Journalists, Build Relationships, Get Details Right*

Put journalists' needs first. If you do not have many contacts yet, start small and do not make demands on them. Look at how other professional organizations are doing it and learn from what works. Even if you have your own distribution channels, journalists can greatly amplify what you do, which is why they remain valuable contacts for you to reach a larger audience.

Build a relationship to journalists. In your organization, have one person who is good, efficient, friendly and relaxed do the relevant work with journalists and media. It makes your life – and that of journalists easier – as your communications officer (who can do other things, too) will develop both the relationships and the necessary experience to understand what is required to succeed. The communications officer should ideally establish a solid library of photos and other visual material, with all the rights, and the social media channels to distribute the information.

Press releases present your organization to the outside world. If you don't have the full internal capacity, you can hire someone to help with press releases from time to time. It may be a worthwhile investment, as a professional can bring the contacts to distribute your content.

Given the high stakes, avoid making mistakes. Make sure you have clearance from your director to publish the release, i.e. give the final version to her before sending it out (this is a way to protect yourself, too). Convince your director that you should have a co-ordinated strategy for public relations. If necessary, brief your director *before* interviews, so that he or she can make the most of the opportunity.

Be prepared for journalists. A good idea is to write down at least 15 questions that you think they might have and research the right answer. Be ready to give them material, including photographs, on what you are doing. If you cannot give an answer immediately, tell the journalist that you will find out and then call back as soon as possible.

Roughly the same rules apply to radio. Television has its own rules, as it relies on images. Make sure you are prepared to meet this challenge before you invite TV crews.

Identify a role model, if you are still looking for your own style. When I was running a research organization, I identified the Pew Research Centre in the United States as our role model, as like them we were doing survey research. The Pew Research Centre had an annual budget that was 30 times as big as ours, and thus could develop templates, presentation styles, and other visual materials, consistently. Whenever we wanted to figure out how to do something, we just looked at their style and adapted it to our needs. One additional advantage of this approach is that it is an instruction that less experienced staff can apply, ensuring a consistency of approach. Check whether there is another institution (ministry, organization, company) that can be a role model for what you are trying to do, and study their work. You will learn a lot by analysing their approach, and adapting it to your context.

Policy or Project Proposal

A document with which you advocate a specific policy or project.

- ***Purpose: Recommending Action, Based on Detailed Evidence – Principle I***

A policy proposal suggests a specific course of action for an organization. The proposal shows what the problem is, what could be done, why it should be done and how it can be done. Writing such a document forces the authors to address a range of questions and thereby helps to guide their thinking.

The written proposal can serve as the basis of an informed and constructive discussion. The policy proposal is circulated to decision-makers and usually to those affected by the policies. All those concerned can examine the proposal and can add their comments, suggestions and criticisms. Sharing helps the proposal to develop as readers contribute their knowledge and experience. The aim is to reach sufficient agreement on the proposed measure and this often entails that the original proposal is modified. Even if this modification is not always an improvement, the increased support often is needed to turn the proposal into a reality.

Such policy proposals can be used in any situation in which you need to address a complex problem. Complex here means that the situation involves various others, cuts across different technical, legal and political aspects, and may have unintended consequences. Planting a tree in your garden does not require a policy proposal or much planning, but planting a million trees in a city does.

In government, policy proposals are used for a range of purposes: to formulate foreign policy, regional health policy or to determine the local repair of the bridge to your village. In institutions, you can write policy proposals to suggest a change in examination regulations of your university, or to propose a modification of room allocation in your hospital. Every modern bureaucracy – whether government or business – works with such policy proposals. The effectiveness of the bureaucracy in part depends on its ability to write, develop and continuously improve such proposals.

Policy proposals overlap with project proposals. They use a similar format. Typically, projects are self-contained units, limited in duration and scope. Projects often are proposed by individuals or organizations to be run by themselves with a large degree of autonomy. Policies, by contrast, can be broad plans of continuous action and statements of general aims that set forth guidelines within which these goals are pursued on a day-to-day basis. A ministry, for example, may have the policy of trying to recruit talented young economists. Within this policy, there may be the project of organizing a specific event to attract an audience that may like to get involved.

Whatever the differences, the similarities are greater as both types of proposal suggest a concrete course of action. Both must be practical and consider how the proposal can be implemented. Policy and project proposals are incomplete if they have not considered this question. Unless indicated otherwise, what I say over the next few pages applies to both the project and the policy proposals.

- ## *Highly Sceptical Readers – Principle II*

The policy proposal needs to be written specifically for your readers. They are the decision-makers and you need to convince them. Tell them what you know and what they do not. To do this well, the policy proposal must be tightly focused and concise. Even if you write about a proposed change in timetabling in your school district, your readers will need to have the information presented clearly and succinctly.

The policy proposal needs to anticipate all the questions and concerns of the reader. Your proposal must be realistic and practical. In most cases, you will try and establish a long-term relationship with your readers/decision-makers. If you deliver balanced and successful proposals, they will develop trust in you. Conversely, if you have given them bad proposals they will be sceptical and less likely to trust any of your proposals in the future. Be sure that your proposal will not disappoint the reader.

To satisfy your reader, you must consider the feasibility of your proposal. Take constraints into account. It should be possible to implement the proposal politically (finding support), technically (it must be doable), economically (it must be financeable) and on legal/administrative grounds (it should not break laws/interfere with anybody's rights). It should be the *best* option, given all constraints. Requiring all cars to be white or silver will reduce accidents due to increased visibility (one study found that black cars are 47% more likely to be involved in an accident), keep these cars cooler in summer, and may be legal and pretty, but enforcing speed limits likely remains a more effective way of reducing accidents. Building more wind turbines in Georgia would provide electricity from a renewable source and set a visual signal of modernization – but at this point, wind turbines remain more expensive than electricity from hydropower, thus they are not a sensible investment, at least not yet. These examples illustrate that there are many potentially good things that don't yet align with policy priorities or political or economic realities. Employ these four criteria (political, technical, economical, legal) to comprehensively examine concerns and to offer the most appropriate solution.

Your reader demands that you have thought through *all* the consequences, especially the unintended ones: what is going to change that you may *not* want to change? If, for example, you propose that the rat infestation could be countered by offering a price for every dead rat that is handed in, how do you ensure that people are not going to start breeding rats? To think through all unintended consequences requires you to be imaginative. Discuss any proposal with several colleagues to develop ideas about some of the less desirable consequences. Play through scenarios on how extreme archetypes – the hustler, the doofus teenager, the beer-drinking couch potato, whoever matters to your policy – will react.

Unless the criteria are obvious, you should state by what criteria you consider the proposed course of action to be desirable. What concrete advantages does it offer? And why are those advantages ("better quality") preferable to the disadvantages ("increased cost") that arise? If, for example, you suggest a shift in school holidays, why is that change preferable to no change? Be clear what makes the proposed policy the best policy: because it has the best mix of risks and rewards? Because it buys good quality at a reasonable price? Because it is the most comprehensive or the least expensive way of addressing a problem? Or because, again, it is a mix of both?

Put in adjectives, many of your readers will be aggressively sceptical, to test whether you have given them a convincing proposal. And they should indeed be aggressively sceptical, because ill-considered policies can harm many people. Thus, any policy proposal should be checked very carefully. (Read the section on memos for reference.)

- *Main Idea First: Action Formula*

You should always begin with a brief description of your proposed course of action. Who should be doing what how when where why? Within a minute of reading, any reader must have understood what you are trying to do. For longer proposals, there is an executive summary that states the main idea on the first page in no more than an extended paragraph.

By way of introducing the reader to the need for your proposal, you include a "problem statement" or "background" in the beginning. This is like the complication in any introduction (see section on Introductions above). With the problem statement, you should define, or frame, the problem in a manner that complements the proposed course of action. Typically, this statement should be quantitative, short and concise. Its actual length depends on the reader – readers who, for example, pay you to solve a problem don't need to be convinced, whereas readers who have not even realised that there is a problem need to be shown its scale and all the adverse effects that they aren't yet fully aware of.

In many ways, a policy proposal again is like an essay. Your proposed action is the thesis. Your arguments will show that this proposed thesis has many more advantages than disadvantages and that it can be implemented. As in an essay, you structure the information hierarchically to help the reader understand. Support your arguments with subarguments – with sound data, examples, references to precedent, quotations, legal considerations and so on.

Whenever discussing potential problems, immediately propose how they can be resolved – or why it does not matter if they cannot be resolved. Ideally, put your solution first ("with this new division of responsibility we can expect agreement from all sides" is more intelligible than an argument that starts "but will not the same counter-arguments by well-entrenched opponents prevent the re-organization again? As experience has shown…"). This helps the reader understand where you are taking him.

- *Typical Format*

Although formats vary, they always cover the same ground: why this activity is a good idea and how it can be implemented.

A simple format can be seen below. An American university uses this format to solicit suggestions on potential improvements from students and staff.

POLICY PROPOSAL
To:
Issue:

Problem Statement
Proposed Solution
Major Obstacles/Implementation Challenges

Signature: Date:

Another, more complex format is this:

1. Background
2. Proposal
3. Potential Obstacles/Issues/Questions/Opportunities
4. Implementation
5. Annex

In addition to the previous format, you discuss how to implement the solution – in the previous example, above, the university administration knows how to implement a good proposal and you do not need to tell them.

Otherwise the overall structure is the same. Since you are proposing solutions rather than describing a problem, the **Background** or Problem Statement should remain short. Describe why the problem is significant, but not more. You want to convince the reader about the quality of your solution, not about the intractability of the problem.

Attention and detail should focus on the **Proposal** itself. Articulate concrete results that are to be achieved, rather than simply an intention to change. Visualize the results that you want to come about and communicate that visualisation.

There are several ways of developing the section on **Potential Obstacles**. You can mention the different potential obstacles under sub-headings. Another way is that you articulate questions that a reader would ask and then give a convincing answer. Distinguish the questions by printing them in bold letters. Following the "Main Idea First"-Principle you can also call this section "Issues" or "Opportunities" and redefine the obstacles as further opportunities.

You articulate the **Implementation** in terms of the action formula: who will do what how when where why. Keep to the usual rules and be detailed and specific about the action. Who, for example, needs to be involved in the new plans? How are they going to be involved? Who else needs to be informed? What IT support do you need? If the implementation is complex and success is uncertain you need to define several stages of implementation. Find a way to evaluate whether your target has been achieved at the end of each stage, and consider some steps that can be taken to meet the target if initial measures do not succeed. What are the fall-back options? Your proposal will look particularly robust if it delivers benefits even if it does not fully succeed.

In the **Annex,** you give additional information that may be necessary but that does not fit into your text. You may include legal or statistical background, some information on what type of data you assembled and what it consists of. If some of your information is based on results of questionnaires, you will include a sample questionnaire. Include a few pages in which you give definitions (sometimes called a glossary) and background explanation that a non-specialist may not be familiar with, if you write primarily write for specialists but want a general audience (including non-specialist managers) to be able to understand your document.

An even more elaborate format for proposals is this:

1) Executive Summary
2) Reason why/Background
3) Proposed Change
4) Detailed Description of proposed change
   a) Problem 1
      i) Problem
      ii) Possible Solutions
      iii) Proposed Solution
   b) Problem 2…

5) How was the Policy Proposal Developed?
6) What will happen next
7) Annex

This format can be used when proposing complex changes that are going to affect many different groups, for example, modifications to banking legislation. It differs from the previous formats in that it deals with several problems, gives detail and tries to be transparent in how the decision was developed. The potential obstacles are dealt with in discussing the proposed solution as the one with least adverse consequences.

Note how the discussion of the problem is kept close to the solution that is offered. The heading "what will happen next" again creates transparency on the process, so that all parties know what to expect. The full legal text, as well as a definition of key terms can be placed in the Annex. If organized properly, such a policy proposal can have more than 50 pages and still be readable.

The format can be adapted to specific needs. The basic structure, however, remains the same. Diagnosis and cure: the problem needs to be articulated and the reader must be convinced that the proposal offers the best available solution according to explicit criteria.

Policy Options

On occasions, you may be asked to recommend different policy options. Again, the structure is similar to the essay and your thesis is that "these are the only three/four/five options that are available to us". You need to show that each of the options is worth considering. It is a bit like buying a used car. There are several options in terms of price and quality: there may be a car that is 10 years old but of good quality and with a price of a $3350, a car that is 5 years old of medium quality for $4200, and a 3 year-old car of lower quality which had an accident for $5000.

In formulating policy options, you should do the same as in walking across the market of used cars. You have to identify what possibilities there are, what choices you have. Identify all the criteria that matter to you (price, risk, quality, performance, etc.) and show how each option corresponds to these criteria. Be as clear as possible in relating each option to such criteria. Be as sceptical as you would be with used cars. With proposing policies and used cars, you venture into the unknown, and only rigorous checking can help you uncover problems that later could cause you much trouble.

Your decision-maker will need all the relevant information to decide which option to pick. The options in most cases will bundle different characteristics in different combinations. They produce different results, have different costs versus benefits, risks versus rewards. To implement a major pension reform, for example, may carry higher risk but may potentially bring higher rewards. A more modest change will have more calculable consequences but may not help economic development (and pensioners) quite as much. To build a solid bridge will cost more now, but will cost less in the future than the less expensive version because it does not need to be repaired every five years. Communicate the trade-offs that are involved. The quality of the eventual decision depends on the quality of information that is made available as the decision is taken. It is worth investing your effort to do this as well as possible.

Give a full portrayal of the advantages and disadvantages of various options. One way of doing this is the ADI-method – advantages, disadvantages, and "points of interest". As points of interest you describe what is interesting but perhaps not obvious about the option. It allows you to include anything that cannot be clearly identified as an advantage or disadvantage.

When providing such options, it may be tempting to present your personal favourite between two unworkable options. If your company sent you to the car market because it needs a suitable vehicle for small errands, you could suggest:

1.) A new Rolls-Royce
2.) Your cousin's not-really-expensive Volkswagen
3.) A 1998 Lada Niva (which still is in Zugdidi)

This trick, transferred to policy options, can work once or twice but in many settings risks professional suicide. If your decision-maker realises that there are other options and that you have not included them, you will lose the trust that is essential to any constructive work relationship. Each time the decision-maker gets a proposal from you, she will be thinking, "are these all the options? What has been kept hidden from me?" – undercutting trust in you. Make sure that you present genuine options and that you do not add further options for ornamental reasons.

Policy Analysis
The policy analysis is a more academic version of the policy proposal. It is often written "from the outside" by academics at universities or research institutes. It does not suggest an immediate policy but broadly analyses policy from some distance. The main difference is that – as the name says – it presents a thorough analysis of the problem first. The Background or Problem Statement is the main part of this

document. The recommendations or discussion of possible options come at the end and are given less space. As this is not a proposal of policy, the implementation does not need to be discussed in great detail.

The advantage of this format is that it can give a fairly objective introduction into the situation. It is popular wherever we want to separate analysis from proposed solutions. Such an analysis can be a preliminary step to working on a more detailed proposal, and can be useful in any large organization, including corporations, or in any complex political social or economic situation. The emphasis is on diagnosis, less on working out solutions.

When focusing your analysis on complex events with several actors, make sure you fully grasp their perspectives, as well as the event's dynamics and the linkages to other issues, such as financial or economic incentives. The cables by US diplomats on WikiLeaks can make instructive reading, in that regard, as they often tie various issues together in thoughtful analysis.

One approach to analysis that I have found useful is the classical SWOT analysis, in which you highlight strengths, weaknesses, opportunities and threats. This analysis is the basis of any strategy: build on strengths, minimize weaknesses, exploit opportunities and reduce (or at least plan against) threats. The SWOT format is also a way of giving feedback which people find acceptable, because you start with their strengths.

Strengths and weaknesses are in the present, and internal, opportunities and threats are in the future and tend to be external, i.e. not characteristics of the organization. Competent software engineers are a strength; the possibility of a cooperation with a research laboratory to enhance the abilities of graduates is an opportunity. The lack of strategic planning is a weakness, whereas powerful competitors are a threat. Or, to apply this to you, reading this section: the willingness and demonstrated commitment to learn is a strength, the availability of good training material is an opportunity.

I have used the SWOT analysis in program evaluations. Here is the table of contents I used for these reports.

1. Executive Summary
2. Program Description
3. Stated Aims of Program
4. Findings
    a. Strengths & Weaknesses
    b. Opportunities
    c. Threats
    d. Overview of Main Strengths, Weaknesses, Opportunities and Threats (on a single page)
5. Items of Best Practice (the best practices I identified, so that people could learn from each other)
6. Methodology
7. Conclusions (reinforcing the recommendations included above)

The recommendations flow directly from the strengths, weaknesses, opportunities and threats. I have included a program description and stated aims of the program in the beginning, potentially deviating from the third principle (conclusion first) because, according to the second principle, the readers needed to be told about the criteria. I have put the methodology-section towards the end, so that people can look up how I approached the task. (In general, put the methodology in the end for all non-academic writing.)

The format of a policy analysis is useful whenever it is not appropriate to clearly state that current policies have failed. By stepping back and writing a sober and diplomatic analysis you can remind decision-makers of the broader picture. You can point out that the original intention has not been achieved and in the last part you can carefully suggest "a policy that may lead to better results". This is less aggressive than a policy proposal that demands a radical change of course.

Executive Summary

Longer proposals should contain an executive summary. Longer here roughly means anything more than five pages, i.e. texts that take more than three to five minutes to read. The executive summary summarises all the elements of your policy proposal. It is, so to speak, your thesis and main arguments. The executive summary is written in clear prose, it is concise and specific. You highlight the main recommendations that flow from your policy proposal. In most cases the executive summary should be no longer than an extended paragraph.

- *Procedure*

The procedure roughly follows the essay-writing procedure of DAGOR. The difference is that there is a tight focus on the detailed proposal and implementation. Also, the setting will be different in that policy proposals often are explicitly asked or even paid for. A problem is identified and then your organization may be asked to submit a proposal to suggest how this problem can be dealt with. There are, of course, economic, legal, historical, sociological or purely practical ways of examining the problem. Whichever you choose, keep asking yourself whether you have done a thorough and plausible analysis of the problem. If necessary, go back and persuade your boss (or your client) to change the description of the problem. It is crucial that you find a right angle to get into the problem. Karl Marx was not entirely wrong when he pointed out that to pose the question properly is already to find the answer.[13]

---

[13] Two books may be useful if you want to get into more details, on policy proposals. Kristin Morse and Raymond Struyk have written Policy Analysis for Effective Development: Strengthening Transition Economies, Rienner Publishers, London/Boulder, 2006, a detailed and practical book. Eugene Bardach's A Practical Guide for Policy Analysis: The Eightfold Path to More Effective Problem Solving, 4th Edition, Sage, London, 2012. His first steps include define and assemble, and then go into more detail.

While you are in the process of working on your in-depth analysis, there is a risk that you will lose sight of the bigger picture. One thing leads to the next and this inevitably is distracting. You should again and again remind yourself of the purpose, the scope and the limitations of your project. To remind yourself of the purpose steers you back to the main theme and the need to *finish* what you are doing – if it never gets finished it can never be implemented. To recall the scope and limitations pulls you away from details that temporarily are exciting but that do not contribute to developing a solution to the main problem. If useful, put the main question on a poster or whiteboard on your office wall, to get reminded regularly.

Typically, you will need to consult or interview other experts. Conversations or interviews will help you to get names of further contacts, information on procedures or approaches to the problem, data in all forms, including statistics, anecdotal or background information.

Normally you begin interviewing after you have completed the first round of DAGOR - you have defined the problem, have assembled considerable amounts of information, and have grouped and organized it already. In reviewing, you have identified further questions that need to be answered for you to complete the analysis. However, there is some flexibility with regards to when it is best to interview. Sometimes it makes sense to talk to experts early, especially to those who have a good grasp of the necessary methodology (and are willing to share this with you).

In preparing the interview, identify the right persons to talk to. They must have sufficient authority and knowledge. Contact them by e-mail or phone and explain your purpose, ask for an appointment. Before you go, find out as much as you can about the issue so that you can prepare specific questions and so that the interviewee does not have to explain simple background to you. If possible, provide the person you are interviewing with the topics you want to cover.

When I was running a research organization, with lots of obligations, I was happy to take an hour to talk to researchers, if they were well prepared, and had read what I had written on a subject, before coming to the meeting. Almost everyone came well prepared. I would expect that many people you want to talk to are similarly willing to engage, if you offer them an occasion to reflect on topics that they find of interest.

In the interview, common sense and courtesy should prevail. Arrive on time, turn off your mobile, don't paint graffiti on the walls and so on. As you begin, you give a professional overview of the project, its purpose and goals so that the interviewee has a good idea of what type of information you are seeking. During the meeting, you keep the discussion focused on the issue, talk as little as possible and do not contradict what the interviewee says. Ask if you can record the conversation. Often, however, this is not necessary. If you know your information well, you do not need to record every word. Taking notes can be enough. If you are not skilled in taking notes, consider only writing down numbers and the most important items, including key quotes, during your interview and then write up the main answers immediately afterwards. Ask for permission to quote and offer to send your record of the interview so that the interviewee can check it. If needed, offer Chatham House rules, in which you can use content but not attribute the source, to allow people to discuss some issues more freely.

It is proper etiquette to send a short thank-you note after the meeting. You can contact the interviewee after the interview and ask her to clarify or expand on what was said earlier but be considerate of her time. If this is possible/appropriate, you can offer to send her a copy of the analysis once it is complete.

Invite the interviewees if you have a launch event or presentation for your policy analysis. Having such a launch event can be a great way to get the discussion going, on your proposed changes, as it brings the interested community together. In this context, remember, too, that in policy research the interviews can already be part of shaping the conversation about potential solutions.

Keep your own notes of such interviews in good order. You may have to use them again later, especially as you compare what different people say. Any important information that you have obtained should, if at all possible, be corroborated by other sources.

Otherwise the type of research you conduct depends on your training and the problem you must solve. There are, of course, many ways to establish valid data. Your research methods must be sound. If you use statistics, you must know how to handle them. There are many training guides (and university courses) that give you introduction relevant to your field.

The main emphasis is on the last step of DAGOR. Keep reviewing your plan again and again until it is right. Have a full grasp of your material and make sure that your statements are correct. Writing a poor essay will bore your readers and may get you a bad mark. Writing bad policy or project proposals damages your professional credibility. The stakes are high. Work with experienced colleagues and co-operate as much as possible. As with any type of document, collect good policy and project proposals and learn as much as possible from them.

- *Remember: Check Abroad, Unintended Consequences, Branding*

As you set how to do research, consider checking what think tank from other countries say on solutions they may have found, or difficulties they encountered when trying to implement solutions. One tool you may find useful is www.findpolicy.org, a search page that focuses specifically on think tanks. I set it up primarily for my own use, but it is a useful resource that is available for everyone, for free. The more specific your query, the better the results you will find.

Before your organization presents a policy proposal to the public, all internal consultation must be completed. Once the proposal has been released, it is viewed as representative of your organization. Consider doing an internal presentation, to test reactions, before you go public. The credibility of the organization depends on its ability to deliver the highest possible quality every time. Rigorous internal quality control is essential.

In practice, you have some flexibility, through a variety of formats. In the British context, the "White Paper" sets out government policy initiatives, often with draft laws, and needs to be detailed and very well considered, even if there still is a consultation process. "Green Papers" in British parlance, called "consultation papers" in other countries, are less formal, do not make binding commitments, and are for discussing policy more broadly. In diplomacy and large international organizations there also are "non-papers" (formerly also known as aide-mémoire), shorter summaries without title or source, to discuss ideas. This format allows new proposals to float. There thus are various ways in which you can put your ideas forward.

Policy proposals can, in some instances, be like memos. The task of both is to communicate recommendations. The specific task of the policy proposal is to suggest direct action. Memos, on the other hand, are internal documents that typically are kept short. Once a memo that proposes action becomes long and detailed, you may want to call it a policy proposal and send it attached to a short memo that will explain what the proposal is about.

Large organizations and bureaucracies often feel that their task is to offer a predictable environment. They adopt a mindset that is governed by three principles:

1.) "We have never done it this way." (To reject a proposal that entails *any* risk.)
2.) "We have always done it this way." (To insist on keeping procedures the same, as predictability reduces complexity.)
3.) "What if everyone else demanded this, too?" (To prevent creating a precedent that others would follow and potentially abuse.)

Expect to run into those objections whenever you propose a new measure and adapt your proposal accordingly.

Be detailed, accurate and precise. You want your policy proposals to leave a good impression. You must know much more, especially background information than you have in your proposal. You must be able to answer any obvious question and should be well prepared when you come to a meeting to discuss your proposal.

Lastly, do at least some branding. When developing ideas or proposals, give them clear and attractive names, implying the solution, so that they stick in people's minds. By creating a compelling image, you help new solutions come into existence.

Report

A document to transmit information.

- ***Purpose: Information Flow – Principle I***

Reports are written to create information flow, so that decisions can be taken. Often reports are collected centrally, then compared and collated to monitor a situation and to react accordingly.

Although the writing of reports in many ways is like the writing of an essay, the nature of their content is radically different. Reports should be written in such a way that it is difficult to contradict them. They should concentrate on incontestable facts that are substantiated with data. The content of your report should, ideally, find the agreement of even those who entirely disagree with your views or interpretation. Or at least, it should find as much as agreement as possible from as many as possible.

The difference to the essay, therefore, is also that you are not asked for your personal evaluation and you are not necessarily asked to present a distinct thesis. Instead reports focus on facts.

In practice, this often is a slippery slope. You choose what facts to concentrate on and this requires a judgment. If you write a report on an outstanding school, you will have to identify which factors make this school succeed. There may be people who disagree with you, for example saying that the success in test results is a result of the vice-director's management experience, rather than of the special educational program. Agreement cannot be taken for granted, as there may be a collision of world-views: environmentalists and property developers are not likely to agree about relevant facts in the first place.

Still, the rule is that the author of the report remains in the background and keeps her views largely to herself. The purpose of the report is that others can make their own decisions, not that the author prescribes the decisions for them.

Reports become most effective when they are standardized. They then are a reliable instrument for monitoring changes and relative differences. Standardization means that the format and style is the same across the organization and over time. The report from Telavi should follow the same format and style as that from Kutaisi. And once there is a format that fulfils all the requirements one should be wary about modifications, because these make it difficult to follow changes over time. Improvements can do damage, as when colleagues once fiddled in a tiny way with how a question on attitudes to NATO was asked, and responses changed, suggesting a change of attitudes when the change was in how the question was asked. Thus, time and care should be taken to develop a thorough and comprehensive standardized form.

- ***Reading Lots of Reports: Your Readers – Principle II***

Reports should be focused, short and concise. They should be rigorous in their analysis and take account of all important factors. The information should be checkable and must be reliable. Information that is not substantiated (you only heard that someone said that...) must be clearly flagged, because the reader needs to know what is certain, established and reliable. Thoroughly indicate your levels of confidence in the information.

The reader will begin to trust you once he has read more than, say, six good reports from you. Up to this point, you are merely writing to establish your credibility. This credibility is fragile and can be destroyed by a single mistake or partiality.

When establishing the relationship with your readers (a good reputation travels, of course), you should take the long-term view. In the long-term, it is desirable for you to build the reputation that you can write objective reports. Even if you feel strongly about an issue and its urgency, you should remain objective and not use a report to try to push people toward your views. (If you want to convince them, write a separate memo/letter/policy proposal/essay.) Once you have established your reputation as being able to remain balanced under all circumstances, your readers will respect your judgment and ask your advice as well.

Yet it can be worthwhile to focus your analysis on solutions that already work. If you were asked to write about the development of agriculture, for example, your reader can easily list 10 problems, most likely without leaving her desk. Your report adds limited value if you repeat that listing. You could, however, do a favour to your reader by looking at the few cases in which agriculture works well already, and ask what one can learn from such "bright spots", and whether these bright spots can be scaled up. Such an approach provides solutions and answers, and can help your readers take decisions.[14]

- *Main Idea: Highlight Critical Information*

As opposed to the essay, reports rarely have one main idea that you are trying to convey. After all you are reporting information, not synthesizing it into one thesis. However, you will state the important facts first. The most important factors will be mentioned early in the report, and you do not build up to some climax at the end of the report. Your paragraphs, as usual, start with the main idea of the paragraph that is then supported by the subsequent sentences.

---

[14] Chip and Dan Heath, "Switch: How to Change Things When Change is Hard", 2010, provides a great summary of this approach. The book is available in Georgian, via Radarami. Alternatively, look up "bright spots" or "positive deviancy" online.

When reporting on different factors, put them into a clear and consistent order as discussed in previous sections.

- *Format*

Always check for the typical format of your organization, or similar organizations. Write a few reports in the style even if you think that the format can be improved. Do it their way before you try to change ways.

Sometimes reports are split: the first section just gives the mere facts that are entirely incontestable. The second section gives an interpretation, which describes the context, causes and the potential development and especially what further signs to watch out for ("if the new production manager like his two predecessors should decide to leave in the next three months, we must replace the General Manager and look for a suitable turn-around professional to get the firm back on track").

The overall format is similar to that of other documents, especially the project or policy proposal/analysis. Consult these sections for details.

- *Procedure*

The procedure works as that for other documents.

The acquisition of data has been discussed in the section on policy proposals. Quantify whenever you can. Consider what data will be most likely to offer valuable information and how you can make sure that the data is correct. Remember that information can often be double checked from various directions. With reports, as with any other type of original research, make sure you keep all the materials and are diligent with your sources.

- *Remember: Choose What Matters, Established Formats*

Effectively, the report overlaps with many other documents. The report can be part of the memo, e-mail, or even policy proposal. As mentioned every report has characteristics of an essay because it chooses what the relevant data is and, if this is not already established by tradition, argues why this data is relevant. If you are trying to learn how to write good reports, write essays first.

The purpose of dedicating a separate section to the report is to highlight that on many occasions you will be required to report on, rather than consciously evaluate, a situation and that your aim here must be to say something that is not likely to be contradicted.

Minutes

How to keep formal records of proceedings.

Minutes are the formal written record of a meeting. Minutes capture the decisions that were taken, and in their more detailed version cover the course and content of the discussion.

- **Purpose: Creating Accountability, Point of Reference, Action – Principle I**

Every effective organization uses minutes. Minutes create accountability and transparency and serve as a common point of reference. Minutes give those who were at the meeting a clear record of the decisions taken, and inform those that did not attend but want or need to know about the meeting.

Minutes help to encourage people to execute plans to which the group has agreed, as they contribute to creating a rhythm of commitment and checking in on commitments. Effectively, the decisions written down in minutes can work like a contract.

- **Curious, Cautious, Nervous and Even Angry Readers – Principle II**

In writing for the reader, you will adapt the minutes to the circumstances and the issues that have been discussed. Where all agree, you can keep to the basics, the concrete decisions that were taken. They should be noted in the action formula: who will do what when where and for what purpose? And, if possible: what is the tangible result and how will we know that it has been achieved?

Overall, readers of minutes can bring a variety of motivations: being curious, cautious, nervous, suspicious, and, in some cases, angry. (Moreover, some readers are historically interested.)

On a day-to-day level, people that have not been at the meeting, but are interested in what happened, will be curious to find out what was decided. They may not have had time to join the meeting because they were away, busy, or are not sufficiently senior to attend but senior enough to receive the minutes. Some of the readers may well be nervous to see what senior managers have decided to do, as their work may be affected. For example, senior managers may have discussed that they want to hire a consultancy to explore a switch in strategy – an innocuous issue at first, but staff members may be concerned about outsiders coming in to give advice, and the potential impact on organizational structure.

In the most extreme version, some readers will be suspicious. They want to see whether the discussion included anything that may become a threat to their jobs. And yet another set of readers may be looking through minutes, sometimes several years after they have been written, to find evidence of wrong decisions, for their own political purposes. As minutes can be politically charged, those who participated will be cautious in reviewing the draft minutes. They will want to make sure that they are appropriately referenced, and that whatever they said is represented in a way that is acceptable to them.

A last set of readers may use minutes to understand how an organization or project evolved, and who participated in what meeting. When I joined an organization to run a project, I spent an afternoon reading through all the minutes of previous board meetings, to get a sense of how things had developed over time.

The potentially strong emotions highlight that writing minutes can be a delicate task. If a full account of the meeting is needed, you may want to record the meeting, in addition to taking notes by hand. In rendering the text, you may still need to find more diplomatic wordings than what was said at the time, as there may be anxious readers, on the outside. In meeting minutes that I had to review in an organization supporting think tanks, there were several examples to illustrate this challenge.

To start with, below was the proposed summary of a discussion on an event that brought 80 think tank leaders from Africa, Latin America and South Asia together. Right on the first page, was this item:

> The peer learning [at the event] was extremely important, particularly for the Francophone group [of think tanks], who realized that they still have to make major efforts and be more proactive to come to the level of the other regions.

In reviewing these minutes, I highlighted "the Francophone group", and said "might some people take exception to this? It may come across as a bit sweeping. Can we find a more general & positive phrasing?" You could read the draft passage as saying that at the event, think tank leaders from Francophone Africa woke up from their misplaced belief that they were at the same level as think tanks in other regions, and now realized that they were not very good at what they were doing. Team members working with Francophone think tanks might find that characterization jarring.

One alternative rendering, not changing too much:

> "the peer learning was extremely important, as many think tank leaders emphasized. Several think tank leaders from the Francophone group said it was particularly useful to learn from think tanks in other regions, some of which have successfully addressed several of the challenges they face."

This version preserves the sentiment, yet changes the framing to one of opportunity, rather than the realization of a gap. Implicit in this rephrasing is the assumption that some people from the Francophone group have indeed shared some such assessment with people who report this view. Based on this, we can make this a statement by some people, rather than a judgment of an entire group. Again, other versions are possible. The key is to communicate the point in ways that are as acceptable to readers (and participants) as possible, while holding on to what was said, rather than cutting it out.

Another example, from the same meeting of international advisors:

> "The suggestion was supported by the group to empower the program officers to 'risk it' and provide honest assessments [on the think tanks they worked with], with [higher] management ensuring cross-referencing among program officers and overall consistency."

In my feedback, I again suggested to phrase the passage more positively. In the draft, the implicit suggestion was that the program officers up to this point had not been empowered to provide honest assessments. This may (or may not) have been an accurate description of the situation, but it carried political risk for those responsible for management up to that point (not me – at the time of the meeting I had not yet formally joined the organization). An alternative phrasing could be "… by the group to encourage the program officers to provide even more feedback on potential areas of improvement of the think tanks they work with…" – in this way, a similar message is conveyed (we want to know more about what is not working) but phrased in a way that feels less like a direct criticism. By saying that one wants "even more" feedback, there is an acknowledgement that such kind of feedback is already provided.

Another critical item was this question, suggested for the evaluation, to be undertaken by external evaluators. Among the issues they should examine was this:

- Look at the failures; for example, for the 3 or 4 think tanks that failed, did we do something along the way that led to their failure?

My comment was "Was that a precise quote? (You can see the headline: 'think tank program wonders whether it causes think tanks to fail'…)". Here, too, a simple rephrasing could be "…3 or 4 think tanks that did not do well, lessons learned for all, including outside partners and supporters".[15]

To be clear, the task here is to preserve the content, and in particular the intended action, while avoiding unnecessary conflict. Often small tweaks are sufficient, such as the ones above: opportunity rather than gap; statement by some people rather than judgment of an entire group; "even more" of a good thing, rather than claiming that a good thing has been absent; lessons learned for all, rather than causing failure.

There may be instances where you clearly need to highlight failures, in the minutes, and for the record, yet this should be a conscious decision. Avoid generating tensions, by unintentionally insulting people you want to continue working with. Bear in mind that some of your readers will be nervous, anxious and potentially even angry.

- ***Main Idea First: Action Points***

The important decisions are best put into a summary at the front. Readers should not have to search for the main results of the meeting. The body of the minutes is for those who want more detail. Use your judgement in creating a balance and keeping the document readable. If, at your meeting, you have decided that the Christmas reception for your clients will be on December 29th, you may want to mention this in the summary.

---

[15] For the full minutes & my comments see:
http://bit.ly/MinutesComment-Sample

Do not need to mention all details ("Giorgi will bring music, Keti the wine, Paata the food") in the summary. Keep it for the body of the text.

- *Typical Format:*

Here is a typical format for minutes, with separate items capitalized:

1.) Heading which includes the Group that meets and the Date
2.) Summary of main action items
   Here you write up the main results to save your reader the time – a bit like an executive summary.
3.) Names of those who were present and those missing with or without apology.
   You can circulate a paper on which people will write their name. If you miss an important meeting, send an apology. Your apology will tell the other participants that you care and realise the meeting's importance. Conversely, they are more likely to take your views into consideration.
4.) Time (Beginning and End) and Location
5.) Name of Chair and Secretary
6.) Chronological order of events
   This order follows roughly the agenda. You list all the decisions that have been taken, following the action formula: who does what how when where why? Only the obvious parts ("in her office") are omitted. Clarify how one will know that the intended result has been achieved and how this will be communicated.

   Another item of the agenda may be elections. The results must be recorded in the minutes and also what type of voting (open or secret) was used.

   If your meeting was formal, you list all the motions that have been submitted and seconded, including those that were defeated, and who submitted the motions. Say, of course, whether a motion has been accepted or rejected. List any amendments that were discussed. Assurances and promises ("Technical officer G. Kureishvili promised that the manuals will be delivered to the departments on Wednesday 15th July") must also be mentioned.

If readers of the minutes need to be informed in detail or the decisions will have important consequences, you mention the main points in the discussion and the questions raised by participants.

7.) Time and place for the next meeting.
8.) Place for Signature by Secretary and Chair
9.) Annexes
This may include the list of those present, reports, including financial reports, memos – whatever your reader needs to make full sense of the content of the meeting. Sometimes the meeting itself will decide what should be included in the annex.

Meeting minutes should be kept in a shared folder, accessible to all people with the appropriate level of authority (and not to others). Make sure they are well backed up, since they represent your organization's formalized memory. While it can be tempting to paste newer minutes into the same ongoing document, it consequently becomes harder to share minutes from individual meetings. Filenames should be consistent, and include the full date.

- **Procedure**

If you are the secretary, take short notes during the meeting. Identify what is most important. Interrupt and ask for clarification if anything is unclear – if you, as the meeting secretary, have not understood a point, others, too, will benefit from a clarification. Make sure you record any motion exactly as stated by the person proposing it. Don't allow people to change a topic without a clear decision (as per the action formula). While not being an active participant, you can help the chair to direct the meeting by keeping it focused. In small groups where there is no chair, the note-taker plays the central role in maintaining discipline. Obtain copies of any important documents (motions, proposals, reports) submitted or referred to during the meeting.

Taking notes is even useful if you record the meeting, as it will give you a structure to work with.

Immediately after the meeting amend the notes, so that you can cover any gaps, potentially still from your memory. Write up any additions so that they are easy to read.

After having written up the full minutes, potentially later, back in the office, potentially consulting any audio recording you may have made, sign them. You can give them to the chair to check. The chair may make practical suggestions, for example to omit specific details of a discussion on the recent poor performance of a firm (or colleague) you work with if this discussion should not be made public, or to rephrase it (see above). Eventually circulate the minutes to the wider group – to everyone who needs to know what has been decided. In more formal settings – larger groups, big decisions, controversial issues – the minutes will be reviewed at the next meeting and then formally approved, as the first item on the agenda.

Keep the tone neutral. Everybody must be able to agree with the way you stated their position. As highlighted above, in some cases that may mean that you find a better wording than the speakers provided.

Minutes that focus just on the results and the decisions can be put together relatively quickly, in less than an hour for an uncontroversial meeting with 6-7 decisions. Very detailed minutes, recording the course of a complex discussion, can take as much as one day per hour of the meeting, especially if the political stakes are significant. An experienced secretary may be able to cut this down to less time, but it can be a daunting task, sometimes involving several team members.

- ## *Remember: Contract, History, Transparency*

Minutes are central to an organization. They are the contract that comes out of a meeting. Minutes ensure that there is a formal record, as opposed to people having to agree with the patchy recollections of the most powerful individual.

Detailed minutes provide a history of decisions taken. They allow you to look back and to find out why, how and when some decisions were taken, by whom. Reviewing these minutes helps you learn from your successes (and mistakes). Minutes make it possible to retain knowledge that otherwise is in people's heads – and vanishes once people leave; in other words, they create institutional memory.

Minutes create transparency. Transparency is good for you – if you think that success should be based on merit. Use it to your advantage. If you want to protest against a decision because you think it ill-considered, dangerous or downright illegal, you can ask that your comment be entered into the minutes. Insist that the reasons why you are against this decision are entered. While such a move will not make you popular, it can help you to distance yourself from objectionable activities.

For your own sake, take notes in every meeting you attend, even if you are not the secretary. Rough notes often are enough. These notes do not have to replace your memory, but serve to support it. (I take notes in every talk I go to, regardless of the topic. Taking notes helps me to pay more attention and process what was said in more detail.)

Use abbreviations wherever you can, for example initials for names. Always write down the date and the participants. At the end of the meeting, review with those present what exactly you have agreed on ("So what you need from me to finish your presentation is X and Y, and you need it by Monday 14:00 the latest."). I myself write the actions that I have to take into a box at the bottom of the page, to separate general notes from specific tasks. Either take all the notes in a small notebook, or, if you take them all on loose sheets, keep the notes orderly in a folder for future reference.

- *Agenda*

An agenda lists all the items that are to be discussed. It helps to organize the meeting and to focus the discussion. The agenda should be circulated in advance so that participants can prepare for the discussion. Advance notice is especially important if complex issues are being discussed that require prior research. Although participants typically are disciplined once a comprehensive agenda is on the table, it is the chair's job to keep the meeting moving according to this agenda. It is also the chair's responsibility to allocate appropriate time to each item.

A typical agenda includes:
1.) Attendance (check on who is present and who missing with/without apology).
2.) Any addition to the agenda?
3.) Review of minutes of previous meeting.
(Do all agree? Any suggestions of changes or additions? Vote on accepting minutes.)
4.) Report by the officers.
(Officers of the company, organization or institution report on the progress made and how the decisions taken last time have been implemented.)

Discussion items (for illustration – initials in brackets indicate who presents the issue):
5.) Finances: quarterly revenues, significant increase (IG)
6.) Marketing: proposed $70k marketing campaign (IG)
7.) Recruitment: re-advertising deputy department head (HE)
8.) Special Project Conference: invitation list (MM)

9.) Any other business (often abbreviated as AOB) – here participants can mention minor points, report on events ("I met Irina from the Ministry of Finance recently and she told me that they found our advice very helpful and would be glad to have us back for another project") or ask questions.

10.) Time and location of next meeting and communication arrangements in between – here the chair, for example, can announce that he will be on vacation, and agree how to be in touch.

- *Procedure for Meetings*

To be efficient, meetings should have a procedure, especially if the meeting involves either disagreements or many people who participate, as when staff in an organization meet to elect their own representatives and discuss their concerns. (Small team meetings can obviously be run by the team leader.) For larger meetings, the procedure needs to be agreed upon beforehand. Usually such procedures are complicated, because one has to make sure that they are not abused. Nevertheless, a quick introduction to the main features of a good procedure.

1.) Elect a chair who runs the meeting. The chair must be competent, enjoy the respect of those present, and have a good command of the procedures. She ensures that the procedure is followed.
2.) Find a secretary to take notes.
3.) The chair introduces the agenda and asks whether anyone wants to add anything to the agenda. If people wish to discuss something not on the agenda, it should be added at this point. The chair should remind the participants about the procedure.
4.) To propose a decision, participants introduce a motion. This motion follows the action formula: who does what how when where why? The motion has to be seconded by another person, otherwise it is not accepted. The motion is

discussed: people take turns to speak in favour or against. A time limit can be agreed and is applied evenly. In big meetings, motions normally have to be submitted some time before the meeting.

5.) If there is the feeling that enough has been said and that arguments are starting to repeat themselves, any participant can suggest that the meeting will "move to a vote". If two thirds agree, the vote can be taken.

6.) Amendments to the motion can be proposed by any participant. They also need to be seconded. If they are accepted by the person proposing the original motion, the discussion just continues. If they are not accepted, the amendment is debated and voted upon. If it is defeated, you go back to the original motion. If it is accepted by the majority, the decision is taken and the original motion is dropped.

At the end of the meeting you can make announcements. It should always be announced/agreed when and where the next meeting takes place.

An example of a motion: "Giorgi Z. and Keti V. propose that the chair will ensure that all future meetings of the staff association must a.) be held on Thursday evenings b.) be personally announced at least three weeks in advance to the committee members d.) be published at least two weeks in advance on the staff association's notice-board. This will allow more members to attend our meetings."

To keep them precise, such motions are best submitted in writing.

Once accepted the motion is a decision: "The staff association has decided that the chair will ensure that..." and will be binding on all.

E-Mail

The instrument that likely dominates your work.

E-mails have transformed modern communication, greatly increasing the volume and speeding up its rhythms. The acceleration offers opportunities but also requires that more than ever you clearly communicate the main message that you want the reader to understand. Otherwise the reader gets lost in a fog of unabsorbed information.

For longer and more detailed e-mails, much of what is in the section on memos and business letters applies. Specifically for e-mail, there are a few sensible guidelines. Make sure that the "Re"-line, like a specific topic in an essay, refers exactly to the content of your e-mail. This helps you to achieve your aims because the person who receives your correspondence knows exactly what it is about. If you are inviting people to a workshop, then the subject line is "press release workshop, 5. April, 19:00 | RSVP by tomorrow", not simply "workshop" and certainly not "Tuesday" or simply "plans".

Insisting on focused subject lines is a good way of getting e-mail discipline into an organization, as staff need to consider what concretely they are trying to achieve, summarizing it right on top. The subject line should contain as much detail on the action formula as needed.

Here some examples of e-mail subject lines as they related to this handbook, and other research and training I have done recently:

- handbook project | needs analysis workshop Sept 29 & Oct 3?
- handbook on effective communication | synthesis of input from civil servants
- handbook on communication | updated draft for your comments attached

- SWOT-report | find attached | potential meeting in July still?
- public speaking training next week | starting Monday 16:00-18:00

The vertical dividing line is an additional useful tool to separate topic and specification or action.

As a conversation evolves, adapt the subject line as needed, especially if you have to highlight something of importance. The hack of Hillary Clinton's campaign in part was due to an e-mail mistake, after the campaign John Podesta had received a well-disguised attack. The IT staffer who handled the issue failed to use the subject line of his e-mail to warn his colleagues about this phishing/hacking attack. Additionally, he mistyped and thus did not highlight that the e-mail which sought to trap the campaign was not legitimate. Without a clear warning, a junior staffer who handled the e-mail account of John Podesta fell for the phishing attack that allowed many of the e-mails from the Clinton campaign to become public on WikiLeaks.[16]

Another occasion to change subject lines is if you want to have an internal conversation on an ongoing thread with an external partner. Putting ~~~ internal ~~~ into the subject line is a good way of separating the conversation, making sure you do not accidentally copy the external party into your internal discussions, and keeping your threads separate.

Main idea first: put the main ideas first, at the top of the e-mail, and for each paragraph. For longer paragraphs in an email, consider introducing them with a two-or-three word summary – as we do in this and subsequent paragraphs. As e-mails are shorter and less formal, they are not read as attentively as letters.

---

[16] This, at any rate, is the account by the IT staffer. See: http://bit.ly/Podesta_Hack (retrieved December 2016).

The paragraphs must be much shorter, because people skim screens, rather than studying them.

Brevity & splitting: try to keep emails short. If you have different topics, with different timelines, consider splitting them into separate emails. After a business trip, for example, write four different e-mails on different action points, with specific audiences, rather than one long e-mail. You are much more likely to get a response, and to achieve the action you intend.

Attaching, exceptionally: if you have complicated information to convey (for example to give a detailed offer), in the past the advice was to attach the details in a separate document. With people responding to their e-mails on their phones, attaching can make things more complicated. Thus, more than ever, try to keep e-mail communication brief, leaving attachments only for exceptional cases.

Action formula & accuracy: while staying brief, make sure you are concise. Just as I am reworking this section, I received an e-mail from a conference organizer, addressed to four academics flying in from abroad and to me, saying that "we would like to remind that we are waiting for your presentations to translate them on time." With this, and no prior communication, we have no idea what "on time" means, resulting in more e-mail communication. Keep to the action formula, "who does what how when where why", to make sure your exchanges run smoothly. Write accurately. Avoid spelling mistakes. They are common in e-mails but make a bad impression. (And thus we end the illustration of how to introduce paragraphs with quick summaries.)

E-mail also offers the possibility of sending mass mailings and newsletters. You will want to do this with consideration and super-edit your postings. For mass mailings, it now is accepted courtesy to put all recipients into blind carbon copy (BCC), though some organizations still regularly lapse. Put one of your own addresses (for example "info@yourinstitution.ge") into the address line, otherwise the e-mail will look naked. This practice allows you to verify that the e-mail did indeed get sent. Newsletter services can be a useful addition, as they allow you to track to what extent e-mails get read and opened, and make it easy to subscribe and unsubscribe. Look around for what is on offer, many services are for free for use on a smaller scale.

In terms of e-mail recipients, think systematically about when to send CC to colleagues and check whether there already is a policy in the organization. If there is not, it may be time to develop one. You should CC if colleagues are actively involved in a discussion or need the e-mail for reference or for monitoring what happens. Putting people too much on to CC results in them not reading the e-mail, i.e. the same result as not copying them at all. If your correspondence only vaguely affects what they do, tell them in regular intervals what they need to contribute rather than asking them to sift out what they need to do by reading through your entire correspondence. As a superior you may ask some of your junior colleagues to put you on to CC initially, so that you can follow what they are up to. But this should only be a temporary measure to train them up to a standard where they can work on their own.

In your e-mail system, you will want to create some system for categorizing e-mails. Personally, I prefer labels, as you can attach multiple labels to a single e-mail, allowing you to give several tags if an e-mail concerns multiple issues. Smart rules or filters often label e-mails as they come in, as e-mails from accounting will mostly concern financial issues. Not all systems support labels, and Outlook still works with a folder structure that is similar to the filing system in your organization.

The superstructure of such a filing/folder system should be standardized within the organization or your department, with some modifications depending on your requirements. When setting up a filing system for the administration of a small college, I had the following superstructure: Admissions, Accreditation, Alumni, Buildings, Co-operation, Faculty, Finance, Governance, Legal, Library, Marketing, Materials, Registrar. Within those folders, there were several subfolders that were adapted by those who worked within the respective fields. Having the overall structure made it easier to locate files and helped everyone to understand what structure we were working in, and respective lines of responsibility. When there is overlap, I put the e-mail in the folder in which it was more relevant. In some cases, however, I copied the e-mail and put it in several folders, especially when the e-mails are part of comprehensive information that should be accessible to others (if it is just for you, you may put it in one folder and then rely on the powerful search tools).

If you are setting up an organization anew, consider having function-based e-mails as your primary mode of running e-mail. This approach is still somewhat unusual, but creates stability within an organization if there is changeover, or people are on extended leave. In this system (widely used in the military, and in some diplomatic services and companies), the e-mail is director@sample.org, and will stay stable throughout. (The address book can still show your name.)

As by now is abundantly clear, you should assume e-mails to be a fairly public document. They are easy to circulate and have permanence. If they are of interest, it is well possible that they will be forwarded and they may reach people that you did not think about when you wrote. Diplomatic phrasing should be the default. You can put sensitive information onto the "soundtrack", i.e. communicate it in person or during a phone call.

Do not misunderstand this as a pretext for not describing actual problems and challenges. The point is that your tone must remain balanced. Rather than writing that two colleagues are paranoid megalomaniacs, you will write "I very much wish that their tone and style had been somewhat more co-operative."

I am quoting from an actual e-mail and case, which we managed to resolve in our favour, primarily by keeping the tone level.

E-mails are so easy to write that one can be tempted to write them impulsively and with a degree of emotion that may be permissible in a personal conversation, but dangerous in a written document. I have seen educated people do lasting damage to their professional reputation because they got carried away in an escalating electronic equivalent of screaming abuse at each other, yet leaving a permanent written record. Always consider how your e-mail may look to the outside audience, or even those close to you: your partner, your parents, your children, yourself in a few months.

One tool that I highly recommend for sending e-mails is deferred or delayed sending. You ideally want to respond to e-mails right when you read them, to get things done. Yet instant responses often escalate the speed of e-mail exchanges, increase e-mail traffic and can lead your counterparts to expect that they will always get instant answers from you, further increasing your load. MS Outlook has a function for delaying the sending of e-mail, and Gmail has paid services for this, too. I try to respond to e-mails whenever I read them, but then delay sending, depending on the issue and recipient, typically sending back the next day. (Your managers may want to have a response sooner, but there will be many others who you do not want to train into a kind of ping-pong on e-mail.) In cases when e-mails need to be written, but are not urgent, you can send them in a week. All of this contributes to slowing down e-mail traffic, thus making your inbox more manageable.

Another tool that is useful for e-mail is a read-it-later app that collects articles to read. If you receive an e-mail with a link (or see a link on social media), you can send these articles/links to the app, get back to work, and read the article later, during a trip or while waiting somewhere, on a tablet or smartphone. Some of the read-it-later apps (Instapaper and Pocket are among the leading services at this point) allow you to forward an e-mail straight to the app, to get it done. The idea is to reduce overload, of either unread emails, or too many open tabs in your browser.

To reduce overload, it may also be a good idea to only check e-mail at set times of the day, every few hours (if that). There is good evidence to suggest that we are more effective when we work to our own schedules, rather than letting the pings of our inboxes dominate our lives. Whenever I have put myself on such a schedule, I have felt that my productivity has gone up. Some tools allow messages marked as "urgent" to go through, or download e-mail from selected senders, such as the boss.

E-mail overload and constant distraction are real problems in many professional contexts. It is worth finding your own workable solution. For myself, I have switched off all notifications, typically do some solid piece of work before opening e-mail in the morning, and do not do e-mail on my phone, except in genuine emergencies. (I have disabled synchronization, and use the search to look for an important e-mail if I need it.) This change felt like kicking an addiction, hard and with regular lapses in the beginning and liberating thereafter.

Precise subject lines, main message first, concise content (action formula), good organization, deferred sending and scheduled download time all can combine to make e-mail communication much more efficient, and are thus worth focusing on.

Social Media for Professional Purposes

Social media mostly is so simple to use that there is hardly any need to provide advice on it. That said, official use, or the use for professional purposes has additional dimensions that may be worth highlighting. Some key considerations below, with the caveat that social media is evolving rapidly.

- ***Purpose: Engage Audience in Conversation – Principle I***

Typically, the main use of social media for professional purposes is to engage people who give you (or may give you in the future) money, votes, attention and time, i.e. clients, citizens, users/contributors/volunteers. The use is more purposeful than the private and expressive use of social media. To start with, being entirely clear what you want to achieve with your social media account is useful. Do you want to prepare citizens for upcoming legislative changes? Do you want them to utilize resources or training opportunities that you made available? Do you want them to use a new service or product? Do you want them to tell their friends and family that they think that your ministry is doing a great job? As discussed in previous sections, visualize the intended result as an action, ideally beyond people just clicking "like". If you're overseeing social media use in your organization, ask your social media team to be clear on what concrete results the social media strategy is driving at, again beyond the social media metrics themselves.

- ***Some of Your Audience Will be Angry – Principle II***

As in other cases, you should again characterize your likely audience with 3 to 5 adjectives, even if the entire world of people online can be your audience (with online translation tools expanding the reach further). With 3 to 5 adjectives you are likely to cover the people that will have the biggest impact on your social media presence.

You are likely to hear most forcefully from people that are angry. They feel energized and driven to reach out and talk to you, or talk about you. Angry people can cause the biggest challenge for you and your organization, even if they are small as a proportion of the people you engage with. Before you embark on a broader social media strategy, and invest resources into it, you may want to figure out why people may be dissatisfied, and how to counter this concern. Do some of your products or services not work quite as people expected? Does your institution stand for something that some people strongly object to?

Analyzing these challenges may be a good idea, so that you have responses ready, and can de-escalate when encountering a public attack. In addition, you may want to set up a channel for dealing with complaints, to bring people away from social media into your institution's established processes. Looking at established practice, it appears that a nice tone, willing to listen and expressing empathy for people who are upset, goes a very long way towards calming emotions. Experienced companies often offer a quick public response of "sorry to hear that, please send us a message at support@friendly.org and we'll see how we can help". How to learn more? Follow companies and accounts that are great at social media engagement.

For public institutions, the use of social media is fraught with risk. Encounters with critical clients or citizens or activists, otherwise limited to one time and place, can become public. This can shift the balance in favor of skillful public critics

People being apathetic and/or overloaded is another adjective to think about. On much of social media, emotional content has more resonance than hard substantial work. Take a former BBC correspondent, widely known for covering some of the world's largest crises. An article he wrote in a prominent outlet, on how some politicians around the world use aggressive rhetoric against women received a total of 10 likes on his Facebook page. The article was a thoughtful piece of analysis, arguably relevant to many of his friends. A few weeks later, he posted a photo of being reunited with the family dog that had run away overnight, a post that received 73 likes. In other words, in terms of likes, a heart-warming dog story receives seven times as much resonance as an analysis of worrying trends around the world. Similarly, a well-known analyst on Eastern Europe, author of several acclaimed books, once pointed out that "only four people liked this commentary yesterday on Abkhazia while about 50 people liked my selfie with a tangerine on the Inguri. This [commentary] is actually more important..." Again, the ratio is more than 7 to 1, in favor of a quick like of a photo versus engagement with analysis.

While "likes" don't necessarily relate to off-line impact – it takes a split-second to like, 10 minutes to read and reflect on an analysis – receiving substantive engagement has to take account of people's overload. It would be too extreme to say that the point is to convey profound points via puppies, but you do have to make it easy for people to engage – again, depending on what you want to achieve.

One good guide to impact can be the SUCCES formula by Chip and Dan Heath. They argue that messages that are surprising, unusual, concrete, credible, emotional and a story are much more likely to have an impact, and that the more of these traits a message has, the higher the likelihood is that it will work. Their book is worth reading, in how to craft powerful messages, once you have your solid structured approach to communication in place already.[17]

Depending on your context, there will be a range of other adjectives to consider about your audience. The good news is that social media can give you data about what works, and what

---

[17] Chip and Dan Heath, Made to Stick: Why Some Ideas Survive and Others Die, 2007, see also:
http://heathbrothers.com/download/mts-made-to-stick-model.pdf
(retrieved December 2016)

doesn't, and that so-called A/B tests allow you to check engagement, by tweaking only one part of the message, and seeing which messages resonate more. The respective platforms will have much information on this, and their own training units as they are trying to sell you on using their tools.

Our normal emphasis on conclusion first is not needed on social media. Social media, especially Twitter, forces brevity. In that way, it has become easier to train people to focus on essentials.

- ***Remember: Role Models, Follow to Learn***

Perhaps the main advice is to identify institutions that are worth following and that you can learn from. US think tanks are particularly adept at using social media, since they want to demonstrate reach. (US public institutions, conversely, are often legally constrained in their use, and thus lag behind other institutions in the policy field.) If you are working in the private sector, follow some companies you admire, and see what they come up with.

Role models may be helpful on guidance for staff members regarding social media use as well. Policies of organizations that are your peers may be a useful starting point. You want to strike a balance between allowing engagement and discussion, and appropriate public restraint by staff members. Staff members do need to broadly identify with existing policies (or products) and cannot undermine them publicly, especially if their profile identifies them as representatives of an organization. Although there are multiple fine lines, courteous and considerate phrasings of opinion on private social media typically works in most contexts. "Personally speaking, I also hope that we will be able to do more to address road safety" is an acceptable statement by a civil servant, whereas "Yeah, my bosses just are not doing enough and do not seem willing to address this issue, even though I raised it often" obviously is not, even though both statements may express a similar assessment. A good test is whether a statement works when it is widely publicized. Taking established policies and adapting them to your own context may be easier than crafting policies from scratch.

As the platforms evolve, they offer new opportunities. For example, in the course of 2016 it became clear that people watch videos on Facebook often without any sound. Within a few months, most videos shifted to include subtitles. Similarly, Twitter evolved to allow people to tag others in photos, making this a convenient way of telling people that you wanted them to know about a tweet, and used in moderation this has become a popular way of increasing online interaction. The platforms will continue to evolve, and seeing participation as being part of a genuine community, in which you learn from others, likely will deliver the best results.

There are significant upsides to professional use of social media, in terms of being available, and being able to engage. Make sure you avoid the downsides in exposure, and in staff distraction, so that you can make most of the opportunities.

Lessons Learned

Capturing what you learn, for your institution.

Lessons Learned, or after-action-reviews, are an essential document for any organization. They distill your experience, and capture the learning that can be applied for future projects, events or processes. Lessons Learned are particularly useful for communications activities, to engage the communications team in ongoing improvement.

External research can certainly support the internal learning process, and support internal politics. However, start the learning process on the inside first, for maximum impact. Lessons Learned is probably the most effective document and technique for that.

Lessons Learned capture what went well, and what can be improved. In a first step, recording what went well helps to make sure that you can draw on similar processes and approaches in the future. Focusing on what went well is a good reminder of your strengths. In a second step, focus on what can be improved. What could you do better? What tweaks could take you even further?

Keep both those parts, however badly (or well) a project went. Starting from at least some things that went well is more likely to engage people in potential improvements. Focusing on how you could do even better helps your team to push further. "Whoever has stopped trying to get better has stopped being good", a supposed quote from Napoleon was the way this was transmitted to me when I was in a training course. At first I thought the quote presented an overly didactic view of the world, but over time I came to realize that it captures that teams are excited when they feel that they will continue to develop.

In the best version of putting together Lessons Learned, the team comes together, with everybody having prepared written notes in advance, to make sure they capture the full range of experience, and do not get carried away by any one focus of the discussion. We start collecting everything that went well, and then switch to what we could do better.

When running teams, I start that potentially tricky part of the discussion with the major things that I want to do better in the future. Hearing their manager talk about intended improvements helps the team to reflect on how they can do better, and gives team-members a positive framing to discuss their own mistakes, and how they will overcome these in the future. The open discussion is a chance for everyone to reflect on what they have done, and helps to overcome defensiveness.

Starting with the things I have learned is a reiteration that anything that goes wrong ultimately is my/the manager's fault: for giving people tasks they cannot do; for not supporting them sufficiently during the process; for not giving them clear-enough instruction; and for not checking in at the right points to make sure things get done well. (If staff members contravened direct instructions, you will typically have dealt with this on the spot. A mistake was still made by entrusting them with a responsibility that they were not ready to take on.)

In this way, Lessons Learned are a psychological end-point for a project or process, and allows people to re-articulate lessons in a constructive way, and to move on to the next stage. The exercises can help clear the air within teams. For the process to be effective, junior staff members should speak up and add their own reflection. This reflection may not be well articulated. As a manager you can help by rephrasing the ideas, to be as salient (and constructive) as possible. In case one or two team members become a little melodramatic on the problems, steer them back in a constructive direction while still allowing for their concerns to be taken on.

Even for big projects, I have found that one hour of reflection is about as much as people can take, and generally covers 80% or more of what matters. You want people to leave the meeting energized, rather than exhausted by hunting down the last details. (If there are technical details that need to be followed up, you address these previously, resolving the issue.)

Lessons Learned should be written up, but can be left in a raw form. I often found it sufficient to collate people's comments, under their initials, and enrich them a little further with additional items that came to mind. The occasion and practice of reflecting, in a constructive setting, is as important as the final product. Ideally this practice of "what are we learning here?" will then continue to be practiced in ongoing projects, and in the way that people have conversations over coffee or lunch.

Leaving the notes in a raw state signals that there does not need to be a final view on who is right. Various perspectives can emphasize different issues, sometimes overlapping, sometimes slightly contradicting. The manager of the next project cycle will need to decide what to make of that contradiction, and can follow up with a conversation. Some key procedural lessons can be put into practice straightaway, for example by updating checklists, or changing templates, or sending some staff member for further training.

Collect your Lessons Learned in a shared file, ideally a searchable folder, that is accessible to all relevant team members, and that you will never lose. This is the distilled and written experience of your team. Doing such Lessons Learned exercises in your communications work will help you get better and better, as you continue to improve details, to achieve the intended impact and engage the audience.

Editing Documents

The section on editing your papers comes last, as all your effort should go into planning the document. I would estimate that every minute you spend planning saves you at least three minutes of editing. Not only are well-planned papers easier to write because you always know where you want to go; more importantly, it can be close to impossible to salvage a muddled document through editing. Such documents need to be taken apart before their ideas are reassembled. Think of the analogy of the house that we have used several times: if the building is a mess because of bad planning, all you can do is to take the house apart and to put the materials back together again. Though planning is hard, it is more efficient to get it right the first time, rather than to correct it later.

A second reason why we mention editing at the end is because it is different from planning and writing. Cognitively, these are diametrically opposed. When you plan and write (in the DAGO or DAGOR), you are mostly constructive, trying to keep the flow of words and ideas going and to put them into the proper order. When you edit, you look critically at an existing text and try to identify and fix shortcomings. That critical stance makes editing a distinct activity, which in the publishing industry is separated into its own job.

Remember to think before you type. Remember, especially, to review your plan (the R of DAGOR) with great care. You should critically evaluate the plan and try to improve it before you write the document. You can save yourself much misery if you do everything to improve the document at this reviewing stage, rather than having to do it later.

Typically, you will edit all documents, and the more important they are to you or your organization's reputation, the more thoroughly will you edit. Within organizations, you may have an internal editing or peer-review process, to improve organizational documents before they are published.

There are four ways of editing with some effect. Three of them have been mentioned earlier already.

> The best editing process is to give your document to others to read. You yourself will have gotten used to the texts you have written. An outsider brings a fresh perspective. But giving your document to others is sensitive and it needs time to develop a culture of mutual exchange and constructive criticism of documents among colleagues. Take the initiative. I myself often give my own papers to my students to read critically. This manual has had several critical readers. They spotted inconsistencies, identified passages in which I say too little, or told me to shorten the manuscript wherever less will achieve more. Through them, the manual has become better. A circumstance in which you always need to let others edit your material (and in which you need to edit it several times to reduce your own emotion) is when you are involved in a conflict. In conflicts, any mistake may be used against you, and when someone is out to get you, additional review is even more important. As I said in the section on e-mails, it is reckless to write impulsively.

Make a strategic decision when to ask for advice: ideally on the draft structure before you write (only applies to larger documents), and then on advanced drafts close to completion. If you have to prepare a large document, consider breaking it into sections and receiving feedback on these sections, so that you can integrate the advice into later sections. Do make sure your draft is in good shape, visually attractive, spellchecked, with page numbers and broad margins creating an inviting space for comments. Giving readers a sloppy draft is a poor reward for their generosity in helping you.

➢ Consider drafting a short feedback questionnaire, asking readers specific questions, to guide their attention. The questionnaire ensures that your main concerns are addressed. Typical questions could include:

  o Which parts did you find most useful?
  o Which parts of the text should be improved? How?
  o What would you like to know more about?
  o What was less relevant?
  o Which sections were most readable? Which sections were most difficult to read?
  o Is there an alternative structure that in your opinion would work better?

Adapting these questions to your needs will help you identify what your text needs to do, and you can begin to answer the questions yourself. Leave space for additional comments.

Another question is to ask readers to summarize what they think your main point is in order to assess whether you're conveying your message.

Also, if you feel a section is weak or needs help, you should ask your readers/editor for guidance. You can either say what you think the weakness is and ask them how they would fix it, or leave it more open:

  o "Can you help me tighten section A?"
  o "I'm trying to convey this perspective but I don't feel I've done so sufficiently, what would you suggest?"

➢ Let some time pass before you re-visit the document. The passage of time helps you to gain distance and to switch into critical mode. However, you only can read the text once or twice before you become so accustomed to it again that it is difficult to maintain your critical distance.

➢ You can force your brain to have a different approach to the document by reading it aloud. Hearing the text will help you discover whether there are any strange sentences or words that do not fit. Reading aloud does not, however, help you much with regards to the overall structure of the document. (The structure, hopefully, should not be a problem after careful planning and reviewing.)

Before you start your editing process, you need to have a printout, double-spaced with big margins on the right so that you have plenty of space on each page. Normally, I would not edit material on the computer screen, unless the document is trivial, such as a short e-mail on a routine issue. Having the text on paper is a good break from the on-screen routine.

A sensible procedure for editing, you will not be surprised to hear, is DAGOR. You will want to define precisely what you are looking for because with the questions in mind you or your colleagues will find it easier to produce meaningful answers (here the questionnaire is useful). You will write comments on the printout, ideally concrete suggestions for changes. Small changes, such as orthographic errors, a phrasing and so on, can immediately be implemented. Assemble more substantial comments separately, including those from colleagues. Take time and group and order them together.

If you have multiple comments from various readers, as I had them for this handbook, it will take careful review to decide which changes can and should be implemented. When you consider substantial changes, you should work with an outline to see how the overall plan is being modified and transformed. The integration of comments may bring some tough decisions. Sometimes you will have to decide against well-founded suggestions, too, but, ideally, only after discussion with others to check whether this is the best decision. Three examples from this manual can illustrate the difficulty of change:

First, one reader suggested that I would need to stress precision. "They have to cut out all the nonsense and have to get to the point!" He is right. Precision could be mentioned on every page. In the end, I decided to include it in the beginning as the fourth principle, when pointing out that you should think before you write. It would have been repetitive and irritating to include it in every section and I decided to say it once, with emphasis.

Second, the same reader suggested that I should include the concept of "Message". Communication (of which writing is a part) is about transmitting a message. It needs to be stressed that a message must be brought across and that you have to ensure that the other side is listening. The critical reader argued that because of the Soviet legacy, this concept of message is not widely understood. Overall, I again agree with his comment. However, it would have been inordinately difficult to include this as a separate concept, not least because it would overlap with the idea of defining your purpose and writing for the reader. I was concerned that the manual would have become confusing if this additional concept had been included. Perhaps I could have made more of this idea if this suggestion had come earlier, before the manuscript was put together. At any rate, it was a suggestion that I did not incorporate.

Third, there is one passage which I personally feel is a compromise: the section where I discuss argumentative, descriptive and debative essays. I jump back and forth and it is not as tightly focused as I would like it to be. Its style is more that of an informal talk in the classroom. The reason for not changing this passage was not so much exhaustion in the last hours before having to send off the manuscript (including the current edition), but rather that I considered it to be an acceptable way of introducing a potentially challenging idea to an audience that is not accustomed to the style of writing essays. It took me some time to make this decision. Reviewing what to change and what to leave often involves compromises.

Whenever you do decide to change more substantial parts, cut this change down into separate small steps. Big editing can be overwhelming because of the unpleasantness of having to change what you previously wrote. Apart from the satisfaction of improving your text, one good thing about editing is that it makes you keen to do well in planning your future documents thoroughly.

- *Minor Editing: Polishing Your Style*

There is also stylistic editing, in which you improve the wording of your document. Such grooming makes your document more compelling, but overall is less important than structural editing. We undertake stylistic edits when we want to polish a text for a wider audience, or to an important partner. A spell- and grammar-check is standard for any document, but we want to go further, making the document more attractive.

The Find-Replace function of your word processing program is a powerful tool for grooming documents into shape, as you can find superfluous words to eliminate or change. The first word you want to eject from your text is "very". Inflated emphasis weakens its own effect. Check each replacement because often you do better by replacing the description altogether: "very good" can become "compelling"; "be very careful when writing" effectively says "avoid writing", and so on. You do not need to be absolutist about eliminating "very" (I wasn't in this handbook), but reducing usage improves your text. You want to reduce all other emphasis (technically referred to as hyperbole), such as "extremely", "absolutely" or other figures of speech that should not be words of writing because they distract.

In a second wave, you can replace other bland descriptions. "Important" often can be replaced by describing in relation to what something is important. "It is important that you remove 'very' from your text..." can be improved by saying that "your descriptions become more compelling if you minimize emphasis, which is why you may want to remove...". The second version is longer, but now we know why we should remove 'very' wherever possible. There is one exception, however: where 'important' is a comparative, it serves as a neat summary – "put the most important argument first" makes a sensible abstract point. "Interesting" is another dull word, best restricted to the comparative or third-person descriptions, since you should "make texts interesting for the reader" and you can only belabour "attractive" a limited number of times. A Thesaurus often finds you the best word.

"Good", "nice" (one friend, when you called someone "nice", would ritually reply "my dog is also nice"), "beautiful" and similar general evaluative adjectives often can be replaced. Again, you will want to specify how something is good ("robust", "stable", "precise", "comprehensive", "well-structured", "elegant", etc.); "nice" (read Jane Austen: "engaging", "friendly", "charming", "attentive" and so on; and realize that characteristics such as "entertaining" do not necessarily mean that someone is "nice"), beautiful (give a visual description that conjures the image for the reader, and again study literature; a beautiful autumn day in Bakuriani will summon crisp air, earthy smell, rustling of leaves, and clear views to distant mountain peaks, fading summer colours; these are merely the most obvious sensations, and they give the reader more than the downtrodden "beautiful").

Some people insisting on English style argue that you can do without *any* adjective altogether by finding the right noun. Often such a word indeed is available, but you need not comply with this advice because it is more applicable to professional authors going for literary elegance who will worry about every word. In a professional context, use an adjective if it aids precision.

Identify your own typical mistakes and cut them out in a last grooming. One of my standard mistakes, partially eliminated, is that I will make a statement and then continue the next sentence with "This is...", which is a clumsy way of writing and overly didactic (which anyway is a major problem for how I write and talk). Escape hatches are to be found by changing the preceding sentence, or replacing "this" with what it refers to, and activating the "is" into a proper verb. Look at the last sentence of the previous paragraph, starting "Often such a word...". It was tempting to start the sentence with "This is true, but...", evoking the clumsiness mentioned above. The phrase I actually used, saying that "such a word is indeed available" creates a smoother connection.

Remember, though, the angry editor who snapped at a junior journalist that "it doesn't have to be right, it has to be written". I myself could have spent another week on this handbook polishing sentences, improving final flow and rhythm, eliminating generalities such as "useful", "helpful" and finessing paragraphs into whatever level of splendour I can attain. But realistically, for professional communication, we will rarely be able to invest the time, since much else needs to get done. The text should be solid, meaningful, well-structured, and does not have to be a work of art.

In grooming, professionalism requires you to read a sentence aloud after editing it, to eliminate any mistake that may have crept in when you were changing word order or cutting a sub-clause. Use the "Replace" function to eliminate double empty spaces as they are footprints of negligence.

For non-native English speakers (myself included, I started learning English when I was 14 and was an atrocious student; as a kid, I pronounced "dealer", from articles on the local drug trade, as "day-allair") standards of sloppiness raise the question: to what extent does grammar have to be correct? As much as possible, is the simple reply. Readers will forgive honest mistakes, especially if the structure of your writing is sound. Yet avoid being sloppy, for example by writing words right once, and then wrong in the next paragraph. In one application I saw, an English teacher writing about peer-evaluation occasionally switched to the edible "pear". In another case, a student (who knew how to spell "and") wrote into the subject line of an e-mail "The main chalenges ahn problebms insavaged in Georgia", four mistakes in eight words. Make an effort and native readers will give you the benefit of the doubt on remaining issues.

One way of reducing editing within organizations, incidentally, is to have a binding style guide, to describe how certain documents should look, how you spell particular words, what type of English you use (US or British), and how you cite numbers or sources. A style guide, on a shared drive to which you can add over time, makes it easier for multiple people to work together, and achieve a coherent look.

The best source on style is William Zinsser's wonderful *On Writing Well: the Classic Guide to Writing Nonfiction*, an entertaining book, exuding both experience and warmth (read it and you will see what I mean). It does, however, require advanced English and the translations into other languages do not work.

Crisis Communications

What to do when things go horribly wrong.

In crisis communications one of your main aims is to ensure that your mishandling of a crisis does not become the focus of the story. You want to make sure that communication supports crisis management, rather than becoming an additional threat to your organization and its reputation. Crises often deepen because an organization appears unprepared and not in control, because it displays a lack of empathy and understanding, and is clumsy in correcting mistakes. The mishandling of the initial problem is often what makes a crisis lethal. Likely, few people today would remember the Watergate burglary if the Nixon administration had not tried to cover it up.

A crisis is a severe test for the leadership, and for the communications team. As institutions can quickly lose trust that they spent years earning, communications teams should invest effort to be prepared.

The first rule is to do whatever you can not to make the situation worse. Within this, the DAGOR principle can be a helpful structure to manage the situation.

- *Define the Crisis – Principle I*

Define what the crisis really is about. One of the biggest problems is that leaders within institutions may not understand how the crisis is framed for the people that are upset. Analyze (3 to 5 adjectives) how the mobilized part of the public see the issue. Once you have fully understood their view, you have a much better chance of addressing their concerns. In cases of police action, in Georgia and abroad, people in government may often see what the police did as a response to thugs (whom they may have much information about, some of which they cannot disclose), whereas angry citizens frame the events as another instance of police brutality, or government heavy-handedness.

In a big flap for the Obama administration, the White House saw a Rose Garden announcement of the return of Bowe Bergdahl after five years of captivity in Afghanistan as a powerful gesture of caring for the parents of US soldiers, whereas angry veterans saw the announcement (and the release of leading Taliban prisoners in the swap) as rewarding a deserter who in their view had caused additional loss of life.[18]

The film The Queen, focusing on the aftermath of the death of Princess Diana in 1997 offers an extended portrayal of how a crisis develops from a clash of perspectives. The British royal family saw Princess Diana as a wayward and self-centered woman whose reckless behavior culminated in speeding at 100+ km/h through Paris, endangering multiple lives and ending her own. From this perspective, many in the royal family did not understand the adoration of the princess, and the public insistence on a royal funeral, when Diana had left the family of her own accord. As the 2006 film suggests, the public in response further romanticized Diana as a marginalized princess, as the queen of the public's hearts, a lonely semi-martyr in juxtaposition to a powerful family insisting on stuffy rules. In a compelling scene in the film, Prince Philip eventually comes around to grasping the gap between the family's view of Diana, and how the public see her.

If there is no Prince Philip in your leadership team, your role as communications professional may be to bring the news to your leaders on how exactly the groups that matter in this crisis frame the challenge you currently are facing. This is a delicate task, in which it is likely that some people will, at least for a moment,

---

[18] It's worth listening to the entire series. The particular episode of the Serial podcast that covers this issue is here:
https://serialpodcast.org/season-two/10/thorny-politics
(retrieved January 2017)

think that you hold the positions that you explain. Explaining people's view within 3 to 5 adjectives can give you a structure for your presentation. If your team understands what it is up against from the beginning, you are much more likely to get the crisis under control.

- ### *Assemble What You Have*

Assemble your resources. To start out with, get the people on board, from within your institution, and from others (for example other ministries). Make sure you have the right political and legal advice on the team. You want to make sure that any step you take is sound, and does not have to be walked back because you run into unexpected opposition or have done something that is not legal. If you do not have the convening power on top, still make sure you connect to communications professionals in the relevant other institutions, so that you can coordinate. Get some of the most thoughtful people on board. Consider getting external advice mobilized. The advantage of an external consultant can be that they can speak freely to your leadership, and challenge them in ways that may be difficult for you, as you will continue to work for your bosses after the crisis. Experienced people often are willing to help for a few days, to get through a crisis, and can bring a useful outside perspective.

Assemble the facts, too. Through the people on the team, make sure you have a full understanding of what goes on, and of the dynamics of the crisis. Make sure you get all the bad news, and ensure that the team has an internal climate that encourages bad news to be shared. Here, again, an outsider can potentially help you to take stock. Assume that there will be more bad news, and that people that should be your allies (other ministers, former employees, industry experts) likely will do things that are unhelpful. Some of your friends turning out to be a problem is part of the playbook of almost any crisis. Even if you think you have all the facts, get ready for more bad stuff happening. Yet analyze thoroughly, before you act. Some people may exaggerate the scale of the problem, which is not conducive to taking the right decision.

Assemble decision-making. Who will make what decision? When and where will they meet, in what rhythm? How will in-between decisions be made? Who has what level of authority, to sign off on statements? Who is your last editor, to ensure that your statements do not have any mistakes, or needlessly exacerbate the situation? Where are decisions made? Get the room ready to serve the team's needs, and put key information (maps, lists, key rules) on the wall, and control access.

Assemble the people you need to reach. Create a list of people that can get your message out. In a severe crisis, offer to sign people up to a specific e-mail list, in addition to Twitter (which is great for crises, if you know how to handle it). That e-mail list allows you to distribute updates, announcements on press conferences, or any other information you want to share. One reason why Georgia in August 2008 prevailed in getting its story out, vis-à-vis Russia, is that the communications group assembled an e-mail list of everyone who mattered, allowing them to push out the Georgian point of view effectively. It was a simple task. Georgia got it right and Russia did not.

Assemble anything I may have missed here. Each crisis is unique, so you may well have additional angles that should be included.

- *Group, Organize, Review and Implement*

Once you have set yourself up, you go to Grouping, Organizing, Reviewing and Implementing, along several axes.

Who does what how when where why? Who is the public face of your communications? This spokesperson should be the same person throughout, who comes across as calm and authoritative, yet also empathetic. Having the same person ensures that you stay on one message, rather than making the public nervous by giving conflicting statements that suggest that you are not in control of events. The spokesperson should carry some clout but not be the most senior figure, as the leadership will be busy dealing with the crisis, and may not want to be too directly associated.

The primary talking point for anyone else on the team is to support the credibility of the spokesperson ("well, we are working to address this issue, and Batono Levan does a very good job in helping to coordinate our public response" – and sticking with that message, until the journalists give up trying to elicit something else).

What is the main message? Clarify what you are doing to fix the problem. You can use the action formula to articulate your response, on what your institution is doing, giving people specific detail. Going back to how people define the crisis, convey that you understand that people are upset, and that you are addressing their concerns, not just solving a technical problem. Stick with the message, and tell your bosses not to improvise their answers, for example by insisting that all statements will be read. Some recent crises exacerbated when senior politicians went off the script, for example by inviting TV crews to a crisis consultation, and publicly expressing anger at subordinates who had made mistakes. Leaders own the crisis, and need to focus on reassuring people publicly, and stay strictly on that message.

(Experienced professionals mishandle this, too. In the case of Bowe Bergdahl, one senior member of the Obama administration had herself lured, disastrously, into discussing Bergdahl's merits, rather than switching to a frame of "look, we are doing this for the parents of the soldiers who serve our country", which may well have resolved what became a heated political issue.)

In your messaging, avoid declaring that anything is over. Let other people decide when a crisis is resolved. Only declare something to be safe if you are ready to let your children play in the affected area. Better, say what your teams have done to make the area safe, and advise people to continue to proceed with great caution, until everything returns to normal. This covers you in case anything goes wrong or has been overlooked. The memory of George W. Bush will continue to be hounded by the "Mission Accomplished" imagery, just as the insurgency in Iraq got going.[19]

What visuals will you offer? In addition to having the spokesperson with clear statements, you may need powerful visual images to convey your message. This could include a site visit by the leadership, to be briefed about the ongoing crisis. The site visit may be an occasion for your leadership to address the public, in addition to the spokesperson. If many in the public already are upset about what has happened, you can use the LEARN acronym to deal with people's anger. LEARN is used by hotels, to deal with angry customers. Listen, and let people talk. Show your leadership listening to those that have been affected. Empathize, on an emotional level. Allow your leaders to express how sorry they feel for people's loss, in sincere words. Apologize, to the extent that this applies. In a political or business setting, you will be careful to phrase this neutrally, as you may want to be cautious about the extent to which you publicly take responsibility. React, showing what you will do. Notify, in the sense of making sure similar mistakes do not happen in the future.

Generically, this is how your on-site statement could look: "We are here to listen to the people that have been affected. As you can see, they have been through a horrendous situation, that has

---

[19] Bush's speech was more nuanced than most people remember, and the famous banner referred to the ship's tour being finished, but nuances quickly get lost.
https://en.wikipedia.org/wiki/Mission_Accomplished_speech

been very hard for them and their families. I can say for myself, and I speak for the entire government/region/city, and really for everyone in this country/city, that I feel very sorry for these people, and what they have had to go through. We are now working on resolving the situation by mobilizing all the resources we have, and we have asked for additional resources from our neighbors, to reinforce that effort. We will also need to review practices, to prevent this from happening again." You can cut down the statement to be shorter, for example leaving out the last sentence, and add detail on what you will do. With LEARN, you cover the main points that need to be made, and have a framework in place to work with.

Another approach to crisis communications, put forward by Regester Larkin, a consultancy specializing on reputation management, revolves around 3 Cs:

1. Care & Concern: express your empathy, your thoughts are with the relatives.
2. Control: what exactly is the organization doing to get the situation under control? "We are working closely with the rescue teams, who are also in touch with the police, and are evacuating affected buildings."
3. Commitment: describe what you are doing to make sure that something similar never happens again. "We are starting an investigation, will analyze the processes and tighten the procedures."

These 3Cs are similar to LEARN, with an emphasis on engagement and empathy early on.[20] It matters that you use some framework, which one is less important.

Organize and plan on how you will stay in touch with the influencers. Keep the rhythm of getting information to people,

---

[20] I have learnt these 3Cs from Stephan Engel, who has consulted many businesses in Asia on crisis communications.

be available, set up a briefing location, ideally in a hotel, close to your coordination center, yet at some distance away, so that journalists do not get in the way, and can get food and drink, as journalists like most people are a little more relaxed when they are well fed.

Get your message to people in your own organization, too (at least to mid-management), and advise them to stay (broadly) on this message on social media, or to remain very low key, so as not create additional problems.

Again, this is generic advice, yet some of the basics are likely to apply in many settings. You will need to review your plans continuously, as the crisis unfolds. Following this advice often is hard – it is a crisis, after all. Some additional considerations may help.

- **_Remember: Prepare, Train, Sleep_**

Prepare for a crisis. Proper preparation is the single most important factor for being able to deal with a crisis, as the experienced consultant from whom I learned the 3Cs has emphasized to me. Things will go wrong. Think of 15 major things that can go wrong, and be ready. Have some key reactions on who to call and what templates to use. Create templates that are versatile. In business, one advantage is that you can prepare for many crises, as many of them are predictable, relating to your products, services or leadership.

Planning for crises may be harder for government agencies because the political dimensions are more complex. Still, plan as much as you can. Be careful on how you phrase the plans. The materials may well leak to the public, through a disenchanted employee, or a hack. You do not want the headline to be that "ministry plans for the assassination of the president", whereas it is permissible to plan for key personnel suddenly being unavailable (for example through an air crash).

If your leadership is amenable, run an exercise, with an external and escalating scenario, for 36 hours, to test your responses, and learn lessons. The questions that journalists will ask in a crisis are mostly predictable, so a good rehearsal is an excellent preparation. In addition to learning a lot, an exercise likely will be a good bonding experience for the staff. After the exercise, write up the lessons you learned, and prepare.

Sleep. Getting enough sleep was one of the main pieces of advice that Tony Blair gave to a good friend when she faced a major crisis. In the beginning of a crisis, there may be the heroic attempt to deal with everything, and keep yourself going with coffee and nicotine. Such heroism can last for two days, at which point the quality of decisions will nosedive. Bosses are responsible for ordering their staff to rest. Subordinates may believe that endless hours are a demonstration of dedication, and thus need to be ordered to sleep. You may need to organize shifts, with effective handovers. If key people, such as IT specialists, need to remain on site, set up a room in which people can go and take a nap when they need one. Keep people fresh, so that they do not make mistakes that make your crisis worse. An exercise for 36 hours will be a good introduction to this challenge.

Lay the lines of communication before the crisis, to people that matter in other institutions. More than anything else, what pays off in a crisis is to be prepared. (Good preparation, for example, prevented a much larger loss of life during the attacks on 9/11.)

As part of preparation, analyze what others have done in a crisis, and how some crises spun out of control. Analyze your own experience. As a team, watch films depicting a major political crisis, and discuss what lessons to draw from it. Again, this is both instructive and a good team building exercise. A team that is ready for a crisis likely is more confident in their day-to-day work, which is why it is an investment worth making.

Conclusion: 4321 To Get Your Ideas Across

This guide tried to give you four principles, three structures, two formulas and one procedure that help you to communicate effectively. If you apply this 4321 framework systematically, you should be able to write powerful documents. By breaking a complex process into discernible steps, we wanted to suggest practical solutions for your personal needs.

You will have to adapt the format and the procedures, as this guide can only cover some of the many possible cases. The principles will help you to decide when this is necessary: when, for example, your purpose or your readership dictate a change of format.

The need for you to make decisions means that your active involvement is always required. You and your ability can always make a difference.

If you are looking to further your skills, there is one practical exercise that I would suggest. Develop a checklist for documents based on the content of this handbook. Drafting this checklist enhances your skills and your ability to concentrate on what matters. Use your checklist regularly, and use it to give feedback to others.

Feel free to send me your checklist. I can send you one checklist that I have come up with in reply. I did not include it because you will learn most if the checklist is your own.

To write good documents requires you to work hard. You should think a lot before you write. Dumai, dityë, dumai. You will need to work hard now to fully grasp the principles, the procedures and the formats. The advantage is that this hard work is rewarded. Once you do it, you will notice how easy, ultimately, it will be for you to write good documents.

Sources & Acknowledgments

To complement this book, key samples are available at http://bit.ly/HandbookSamples. The list of samples includes documents that I have written over the years, using these techniques, and may be useful to review.

This handbook was written part from practical experience (in academia, advocacy, fundraising, project management, higher education management and business), part by examining current practice and by asking experienced practitioners.

In this current version, the handbook has been made possible by Mary Gabashvili and Natalie Nozadze in Tbilisi. Special thanks to them.

In preparing this third edition, I am grateful to several people. Stephan Engel shared experience of working on crisis communications for companies throughout Asia. Andrew Bennett gave extremely useful advice on press releases. Teaching how to write essays, at the University of Bamberg, has refined my understanding of how to pitch these skills, and I want to especially thank Christian Illies and Manuel Gebhardt for all I have learned from working there and with them, for many years. I have learned a lot from my colleagues at Transparify, from the supreme pragmatism of Tinatin Ambroladze, and from the great instinct for good communications by Till Bruckner. Jennifer Lappin provided some excellent comments.

For previous editions, I want to thank Mark Mullen and Tamar Karosanidze who came up with the idea for this handbook when they were at Transparency International - Georgia, way back when; Salome Tsereteli, Kote Vekua, and Nino Dzotzenidze at AFP (back then), all in Tbilisi; Andreas Tiegelkamp and Kevin Canty in Berlin, as well as countless students. Maggie Osdoby Katz has been an attentive reader, providing valuable guidance to the second edition. John Mason's suggestions on how students should develop theses transformed my thinking and I have adapted his suggestion for this book. Special thanks to my parents, Marianne and Karl Gutbrod. My father has been a great teacher on these matters, sharing his experience in business in multiple countries. Shared as the credit is, the responsibility for any remaining lapses is mine.

Additionally, I would like to mention translators and editors: Miranda Berishvili and Nana Danelia in Tbilisi; Krasimira Miteva in Varna, Bulgaria; Ulziibayar Vangansuren in Ulan Baator, Mongolia; Alexander Byelyakov in Kyiev, Ukraine; Meruzhan Galstyan in Yerevan, Armenia. I have also learnt much from working with Boris Adamovich, in Colombia, who adapted and translated part of this handbook into Spanish. Effectively, all of them were co-authors, adapting the content to their own countries and giving feedback which I integrated in this edition.

I reviewed lots of internet material, little of which as useful as I would have hoped which is why I didn't mention any web sites. There are five books that I would like to recommend. One book that provided an important inspiration was Barbara Minto, *The Pyramid Principle*, Prentice Hall, London, 1995. It is the best summary I have found of how to order ideas logically. Another outstanding book offering advice about planning -- which is what good writing is about -- is by Richard Stutely, *The Definitive Business Plan*, Prentice Hall, London, 1999. The best book on style in English, as previously mentioned, is William Zinsser's *On Writing Well: the Classic Guide to Writing Nonfiction*, HarperCollins, New York, 2001, though it is primarily written for an American audience. Edward Tufte has written a remarkable series of books, with the most important being *The Visual Display of Quantitative Information*, Graphics Press, Cheshire, Connecticut, 2001. Chip and Dan Heath, *Made to Stick* is an excellent book on how to craft compelling messages. It is a great book to read if you already know how to structure information. I don't think you need any more books about communication, although it helps if you remain curious.

For non-native speakers who try to improve their formal English, I recommend John Swales and Christine Feak, *Academic Writing for Graduate Students: a Course for Non-Native Speakers of English*, University of Michigan, Ann Arbor, 2004. It includes many practical exercises and suggestions on nuances of grammar and expression, for example in how to express degrees of confidence. Although primarily aimed at graduate students, it will help people who need to write professionally in a language that is not their mother tongue.

Mainly I want to thank all the Georgians who I have worked with over the years. It is to all of them that this book is dedicated.

Follow me on Twitter http://bit.ly/Twitter_HG or send me an e-mail to hfgutbrod+subscribe@gmail.com, to receive my occasional newsletter on communications. In case you want advice on how to integrate these practices in an organization, please write to hfgutbrod@gmail.com.

Hans Gutbrod works in policy research and policy advocacy, in diverse fields. With Transparify, he convinced dozens of think tanks around the world to become more transparent on their funding sources. He has worked with think tanks in Latin America, Africa and South Asia, and for many years worked as the Regional Director of the Caucasus Research Resource Centers. Prior to this, he taught and trained at various institutions. Hans was born in Brazil, grew up in Germany and studied in Tübingen and at the London School of Economics, where he obtained his Doctorate in International Relations.